D0260115

LUKE

New Hope,
New Joy

26 studies in 2 parts
for individuals or groups

Ada Lum

With Notes for Leaders

Scripture Union is an international Christian charity working with churches in more than 130 countries providing resources to bring the good news about Jesus Christ to children, young people and families – and to encourage them to develop spiritually through the Bible and prayer. As well as a network of volunteers, staff and associates who run holidays, church-based events and school Christian groups, Scripture Union produces a wide range of publications and supports those who use their resources through training programmes.

Scripture Union, 207-209 Queensway, Bletchley, MK2 2EB, UK.
e-mail: info@scriptureunion.org.uk
www.scriptureunion.org.uk

Scripture Union Australia: Locked Bag 2, Central Coast Business Centre, NSW 2252.
www.su.org.au

ISBN 1 85999 487 3

First published in the United States by InterVarsity Press.
Published in Great Britain by Scripture Union in 2002, reprinted 2003, 2004, 2006.

Printed in Great Britain by goodmanbaylis, The Trinity Press, Worcester and London.

Contents

PART 2: THE WAY TO JERUSALEM
LUKE 9:51—24:53

Getting the Most
Out of *Luke*

As kids, when we said, "I hope so," we would cross our fingers or knock on wood, as though the outcome depended on luck. That is our human dilemma. We have an instinct that life can be better than it is in the present. We hope and work for that goal. But there lurks within us a feeling that maybe it isn't going to happen. Security and happiness seem like morning mists.

Scripture tells us that hope does not have to be an illusion. It is God's pure intent that we should be secure and happy. The problem is that we work for it in our limited ways instead of living and working with God in his liberating ways.

Time and again I've seen that people discover new hope and new joy as they personally relate to the real Jesus of the Gospels.

An Interview with Dr. Luke

The following imaginary interview of Luke, the writer, by Lydia, a merchant of Philippi, is based on Acts 16:6-40; 20:5—28:31 (the "we" passages where the writer of Acts includes himself in Paul the apostle's missionary team); Colossians 4:14; 2 Timothy 4:11 and Philemon 24.

Ms. Lydia: Congratulations on the publication of your Gospel, Dr. Luke! The first thing our Philippian church observed was its length—just about twice Mark's Gospel. You fill up the curiosity gaps in his account of Jesus' life, like Jesus' birth and childhood and that third-year trip to Jerusalem in chapters 9 to 19. Were you familiar with Mark's Gospel when you wrote yours?

Dr. Luke: Oh yes. Mark was a great help in my research. He wrote for Romans, and you know how they like fast-moving action, not too much abstract teaching. I wrote for Theophilus and his friends. Some are high-ranking government officials who are new or not-yet believers. They want to see the big picture, lots of concrete evidence, human relevance. By the way, that's why in both my Gospel and the book of Acts, I include prominent people who were attracted to Jesus. My friends can identify with them in one way or another.

Ms. Lydia: We Philippians appreciate your including many foreigners, social outcasts and unique women. It's clever how you begin your Gospel with a couple (1:5-25) and end with another couple (24:13-35). And we love your humor that pops up every now and then, for instance, in the Zacchaeus story (19:1-10).

Dr. Luke: Humour? Ah, yes. Jesus' pleasant sense of the unexpected rubbed off on me. Peter and the other disciples used to recount funny stories Jesus told in their evening relaxation. They also would point out in his teachings how he described human nature with a knowing twinkle in his eyes. And children loved him! He knew how to be playful with them.

Ms. Lydia: You amaze me. You're the only one of the Gospel writers who did not meet Jesus in the flesh. Yet he seems so personally real to you.

Dr. Luke: Initially I was first intrigued with Jesus as the ideal Philosopher King that our Greek philosophers have been searching for. But the longer I researched his history, the more I met men and women who had personally known him and were transformed by him. I also met people who never met him physically but were also transformed! Could Jesus be more than an ideal man?

Ms. Lydia: When did you begin such thorough research about Jesus?

Dr. Luke: Just before I met you women in your prayer meeting at the river Gangites. I had met the apostle Paul and his missionary team in Troas, where I was purchasing medical supplies. Paul saw that I was interested in the new religion turning the world upside down. So he spent hours—days!—telling me about Jesus and the vast implications of his life, death and resurrection. When it was time for my ship to leave for Macedonia, I persuaded him and his team that a great mission field lay in our region and the rest of Europe. Rather, the Holy Spirit persuaded them.

Ms. Lydia: You learned fast about the Way. We were delighted that Paul left you behind to pastor our new church in Philippi. Why, you were the key to opening up Europe to Christianity! We were sad when you later left to rejoin him and the team. But that's the nature of our faith, isn't it? Keep spreading the good news of Jesus. Your Gospel will go a long way to do that too. What is the aim in your version of the Jesus story?

Dr. Luke: My prayer is that Theophilus, his friends and other readers will be drawn to Jesus as a strong, compassionate friend and a person who speaks across cultural boundaries. Jesus is the kind of person they themselves long to be—fully alive, fully human.

Two General Tips on Reading Luke's Gospel

The first tip is to get into the picture yourself. It's the you-are-there principle of imagining you are part of the crowd listening to Jesus, the new preacher in town. Or you're Simon Peter resisting Jesus' foolish instructions. Or the widow whose only son has died. Or Jesus himself, rejected by his hometown and misunderstood by his family. Develop this skill of identifying with biblical characters, and the Bible will become more alive to you.

The second tip is constantly to see Luke's big picture of Jesus' life and mission. Watch how and why he links together certain events and teachings. We can readily see this in the early chapters because of the chronological sequence of Jesus' birth, childhood and the opening events of his ministry (chaps. 1-4). But in the next chapters, sequence of theme may not be as obvious. For instance, some commentators believe that the teachings and healing story in 17:1-19 are miscellaneous, unrelated. But see study nineteen for a suggested integration of these texts and their context.

Again, the marvelous story of Jesus' encounter with a prostitute and a Pharisee at the same time in the same house can stand by itself (7:36-50). But it is actually Luke's live illustration of Jesus' preceding teaching on who really qualifies for the kingdom of God (7:29-35). Looking for the writer's progression helps you see the big picture. A fascinating videotape of *Jesus Alive!* will replace your photo album of favourite Jesus photos.

Suggestions for Individual Study

1. As you begin each study, pray that God will speak to you through his Word.

2. Read the introduction to the study and respond to the "personal reflection" question or exercise. This is designed to help you focus on God and on the theme of the study.

3. Each study deals with a particular passage—so that you can delve into the author's meaning in that context. Read and reread the passage to be studied. If you are studying a book, it will be helpful to read through the entire book prior to the first study. The questions are written using the language of the New International Version, so you may wish to use that version of the Bible. The New Revised Standard Version is also recommended.

4. This is an inductive Bible study, designed to help you discover for yourself what Scripture is saying. The study includes three types of questions. *Observation* questions ask about the basic facts: who, what, when, where and how. *Interpretation* questions delve into the meaning of the passage. *Application* questions help you discover the implications of the text for growing in Christ. These three keys unlock the treasures of Scripture.

Write your answers to the questions in the spaces provided or in a personal journal. Writing can bring clarity and deeper understanding of yourself and of God's Word.

5. It might be good to have a Bible dictionary handy. Use it to look up any unfamiliar words, names or places.

6. Use the prayer suggestion to guide you in thanking God for what you have learned and to pray about the applications that have come to mind.

7. You may want to go on to the suggestion under "Now or Later," or you may want to use that idea for your next study.

Suggestions for Members of a Group Study

1. Come to the study prepared. Follow the suggestions for individual study mentioned above. You will find that careful preparation will greatly enrich your time spent in group discussion.

2. Be willing to participate in the discussion. The leader of your group will not be lecturing. Instead, he or she will be encouraging the members of the group to discuss what they have learned. The leader will be asking the questions that are found in this guide.

3. Stick to the topic being discussed. Your answers should be based on the verses which are the focus of the discussion and not on outside authorities such as commentaries or speakers. These studies focus on a particular passage of Scripture. Only rarely should you refer to other portions of the Bible. This allows for everyone to participate in in-depth study on equal ground.

4. Be sensitive to the other members of the group. Listen attentively when they describe what they have learned. You may be surprised by their insights! Each question assumes a variety of answers. Many questions do not have "right" answers, particularly questions that aim at meaning or application. Instead the questions push us to explore the passage more thoroughly.

When possible, link what you say to the comments of others. Also, be affirming whenever you can. This will encourage some of the more hesitant members of the group to participate.

5. Be careful not to dominate the discussion. We are sometimes so eager to express our thoughts that we leave too little opportunity for others to respond. By all means participate! But allow others to also.

6. Expect God to teach you through the passage being discussed and through the other members of the group. Pray that you will have an enjoyable and profitable time together, but also that as a result of the study you will find ways that you can take action individually and/or as a group.

7. Remember that anything said in the group is considered confidential and should not be discussed outside the group unless specific permission is given to do so.

8. If you are the group leader, you will find additional suggestions at the back of the guide.

1

People of Hope

Luke 1

The couple in California made front-page news. They were in their mid-sixties, and she was expecting their first child! A week later we saw a photo of the fine-looking immigrant couple from the Philippines and their beautiful baby daughter. After forty years their dreams came true.

GROUP DISCUSSION. What thoughts rush into your mind as you consider the story of the California couple?

PERSONAL REFLECTION. Think of an extraordinary personal experience that you could not account for apart from God's unique intervention. What bigger view of God did you learn from that?

Luke begins his Gospel with sensational news. For over four hundred years God's people have heard no prophetic voice. The people wonder, Has God forgotten us? Has he reneged on his many promises to send Messiah to deliver us? No. God is about to break through Israel's darkness with powerful light, and he does this through very unlikely people—an elderly, childless couple and a teenage girl engaged to a peasant carpenter. *Read Luke 1:5-25.*

---

1. God chose this elderly couple for an extraordinary job. Several factors in verses 5-10 give hints of God's reasons for this choice. What might those reasons be?

2. For better or for worse, angels have recently become quite popular. But in what ways is the angel here different from how angels are depicted in popular culture (vv. 11-17)?

3. Do you find yourself sympathetic or critical of Zechariah's response of unbelief (vv. 18-22)? Explain your view.

4. The circumstances of the birth of the Messiah's forerunner were very unusual. Why do you think God wanted this particular birth to be unusual?

5. *Read Luke 1:26-56* for Gabriel's second birth announcement. In what ways is it even more extraordinary than the first?

6. How would you compare and contrast Mary and Zechariah's responses?

7. Which would you find easier to believe—a promise from God through an angel or a promise through the Bible? Why?

8. From Mary's song of response (vv. 46-55), how does your concept of God compare with hers?

9. *Read Luke 1:57-80.* Note that Luke describes people's spontaneous reactions to John's birth three times. What might be Luke's purpose in repeating this fact?

10. The Holy Spirit has sharpened Zechariah's faith to see (1) the great acts that God's Redeemer will do (vv. 68-75) and (2) his child's unique relation to this Redeemer (vv. 76-79). Suppose you were one of the neighbors listening to his prophecy. As a devout Jew, which part would have especially stirred you? Explain.

11. Zechariah and Mary expressed their hope in God differently. What in their interaction with God gives you hope as you also seek to trust God totally?

Thank God for being the only source of true hope.

Now or Later

Luke records Jesus' birth with Mary's perspective. Consider Joseph's perspective in Matthew 1:18-24; 2:13-16, 19-23. Jesus' adoptive father also had unique faith! What did he go through?

To expand your angelology: Hebrews 1 gives an overall understanding of angels (to people who then were tempted to worship them). See especially verse 14. They were active throughout the Old Testament. They witnessed creation (Job 38:7), destroyed evildoers (Genesis 19:1ff.), have warlike potential (Genesis 32:1-22), restrained a false prophet (Numbers 22:21-35), mediated God's law to Moses (Acts 7:38, 53), served as God's messengers (Judges 6:11-23), aided his servants (1 Kings 19:5-7), gave military assistance (2 Kings 19:35). They strengthened Jesus in temptation (Mark 1:13; Luke 22:43) and were present at his resurrection and ascension (Luke 24:4-7; Acts 1:9-11). They guided the apostles in evangelization (Acts 8:26; 10:3-8; 12:7-10; 27:23).

2

Child of Hope

Luke 2

Did you hear the one about the shopper at Christmas who came upon a nativity scene in a department store? When she saw the figurines of Mary, Joseph, the shepherds and the wise men surrounding Jesus, she exclaimed in disgust, "Now look what they're dragging into Christmas: religion!" That's where many are in their understanding of Christmas. But we all need a fresh view of this momentous turning point in history.

GROUP DISCUSSION. What do you like best about Christmas?

PERSONAL REFLECTION. Don't let the world take away the awesome wonder of this turning point in our human history. With your resources, what can you do to retain or nurture this holy wonder?

Luke anchors Jesus' birth in history, in the powerful world of Rome. *Read Luke 2:1-20.* Try seeing the unfolding scenes through the wonder-filled eyes of a child.

---

1. Think of the inconveniences that Caesar's census brings. How would it have felt to be Joseph on that weeklong walk from Nazareth to Bethlehem?

How would Mary have felt?

2. Luke's account of Jesus' birth reads like a newspaper article (vv. 6-7). What overall impression does the writer leave with you?

3. We put shepherds on our Christmas cards and in our pageants. But back then they were an outcast group. What in the angels' message would be incredible to them (vv. 9-14)?

4. From what you have seen of Mary and Joseph so far, what character qualities do you notice?

5. *Read Luke 2:21-50.* These verses include prophetic events about this child of hope. The first one focuses on Jesus' name (v. 21). The second and third prophetic events are closely tied together (vv. 22-38). What do you find unusual about Simeon?

about Anna?

6. Simeon's prophecy is much longer than Anna's. But what do they both see about the infant?

7. The fourth prophetic event tells us much about Jesus' growing awareness of himself and of his relationship to others. What do you learn about him in his meeting with the nation's top biblical scholars (vv. 46-47)?

What more do you discover about Jesus from his response to Mary's rebuke (vv. 48-50)?

8. Luke is eager to portray the boy Jesus as a normal child, developing as a well-rounded human person (vv. 40, 51-52). In which of these areas do you need growth to be a well-rounded person like Jesus?

What steps will you take to achieve this?

It wasn't easy for Jesus to become a well-rounded person; it won't be easy for you. But he will help you do it. Ask him.

Now or Later

People can err on two extremes in their view of Mary. One extreme exalts her as comediator with Jesus. The other extreme totally ignores her unique place in God's history. References beyond Luke 1—2 are few but give a more balanced picture (in chronological order): John 2:1-5; Mark 3:31-35; John 19:26-27; Acts 1:14.

The temple and its rituals in Jerusalem were significant to Mary and Joseph and increasingly so to Jesus. So was the local synagogue, the center of any Jewish community. He most likely attended the Nazareth synagogue school, as did most Jewish boys. Later in his ministry Jesus went to the synagogue on the sabbath "as was his custom." Visit a synagogue in your community. You will be enriched.

3

Preacher of Hope

Luke 3:1-20

Some years ago, before Queen Elizabeth arrived in a British Commonwealth country, its people feverishly prepared a royal welcome. They paid special attention to the highway running from the airport to the capital. The government gave paint to each house along that route, but only enough to cover the front of the house!

When it comes to our own repentance, a change of mind, a 180-degree reversal of attitude toward sin, God does not ask for cosmetic changes. He calls for changes inside and outside, all the way to the back door.

GROUP DISCUSSION. Repentance is not a common subject from our pulpits. What are possible reasons?

PERSONAL REFLECTION. When was the first time you deeply repented of sin and then knew God's forgiveness?

In this passage we meet John the Baptizer calling for repentance. *Read Luke 3:1-20.*

---

1. How are the authorities described in verses 1–2 different from John?

What do you think Luke wants to reveal through this contrast?

2. Now to John's preaching of repentance (vv. 3-9). Some think that talk about repentance is negative. But by insisting on it, John is a positive preacher of hope. What connection can you see between repentance and hope?

3. "A brood of vipers" is what John calls his listeners. Yet they respond positively to his message! How would you respond if some preacher called your church a brood of vipers?

4. Three representative groups respond to John's passionate appeal and ask what they should do. Compare his three answers. In all three cases, what basic sin is he attacking (vv. 8-14)?

What injustices in your community are similar to those in John's day?

5. How does John contrast his ministry with the ministry of the Christ (vv. 15-18)?

6. Like repentance, judgment is not a popular topic today among many Christians. How could you explain to such people that judgment is part of the good news (v. 18)?

7. Churches are sometimes criticized for having preachers who are either wimps or fire-breathing evangelists. What kind of preacher appeals to you?

---

8. Powerful, effective preachers like John are not produced overnight. Look back at 1:13-15 and 1:80. What factors shaped John's character?

How can our churches help produce preachers like John for our day?

---

9. Repentance is a message we all need to hear. In your own words, how would you explain what repentance is?

Pray for yourself or for a seeker who needs to understand repentance.

Now or Later

Notice John's humility in verses 15-17. What can help us to have humility like John's? True humility is not the same as an inferiority complex. Nor is it a gift of the Holy Spirit! Humility begins with the proper view of God (Isaiah 57:15). See what else you can learn about this rare virtue from Proverbs 16:19; 22:4; 29:23; Romans 12:3; Philippians 2:5; James 4:10 and 1 Peter 5:5. And consider what Jesus himself taught about humility in Matthew 18:4.

4

Hope for All People

"The best way to get rid of temptation is to give in to it," said Oscar Wilde. He was the brilliant, flamboyant Irish writer of the second half of the nineteenth century. He died young, gifted and dissipated by his unbridled passions.

GROUP DISCUSSION. What realities must we consider in setting major goals for our life?

PERSONAL REFLECTION. What goal would you like to have achieved ten years from now?

Like Oscar Wilde, Jesus died young and gifted, but disciplined by his passion for his Father God. His discipline began in childhood with an early consciousness of his life mission. Now at thirty he submits himself to more disciplines to further prepare him for this goal. *Read Luke 3:21-23*, noting that this is Jesus' first public appearance.

1. Luke's brief account of Jesus' baptism focuses on Jesus' hidden identity. What would this "public announcement" do for Jesus as he begins his ministry?

2. At thirty Jesus had already made crucial choices about occupation,

family ties and home life. Think of hard choices you have made. How have they shaped your life?

3. Luke's genealogy of Jesus begins with Joseph. It reaches all the way to "Adam, the Son of God" (3:23-38). Luke is stressing not Jesus' ethnic genealogy (as does Matthew) but his humanness. Reflect on this: Jesus is one of us! How does this deepen your appreciation of him?

What questions does it possibly raise for you?

4. *Read Luke 4:1-13.* Temptations are not the same as sins. Temptations are strong appeals to satisfy legitimate desires in wrong circumstances, with wrong means, for wrong motives. In each appeal to Jesus, what natural desire is the devil trying to get him to satisfy?

5. God built these natural desires into all of us. Why would it have been wrong if Jesus had satisfied each desire in those circumstances?

6. What would be involved for you to be prepared to resist some of the temptations you face?

7. Jesus' temptations appear to have little resemblance to ours. Yet Hebrews 4:15 tells us he "has been tempted in every way, just as we are." Think of your fiercest temptation. In what way is it like one of Jesus' temptations?

8. If we want to serve God wholeheartedly, we too must undergo tough training. In which area do you feel the greatest need for discipline?

What could be your first step in that direction?

What temptation have you been struggling with? Turn to Jesus now. He's waiting.

Now or Later

Some Christians believe that Jesus could never have sinned because he was God or that it was a snap for him to resist temptations. That would make his thirty-three years on earth a farce—God pretending to be a man! If that were so, how could he be a model of life for us? Moreover, how could his death be a true substitute for ours? Check these Scriptures to help you answer these questions: 1 Corinthians 5:21; Philippians 2:5-11; Hebrews 2:8-18; 5:7-10.

As long as we are in earthly bodies we have to live with temptations. Jesus' example should inspire us. For further study reflect more on Hebrews 2:14-18. See also 1 Corinthians 10:13; Hebrews 4:14-16; James 1:13-15 and Joseph's example in Genesis 39. What happens to your character when you get into the habit of saying no to the devil?

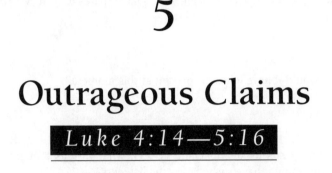

5

Outrageous Claims

Luke 4:14—5:16

Monarchies in the west are becoming a source of gossip and ridicule. Those elsewhere are questionable in other ways. Most of us like living in a democracy where the people rule. Democracies are imperfect, but they are the best form of government—on earth. If, however, you're expecting to go to heaven, it's a good idea to learn to live in a monarchy. In God's kingdom, God, not the majority, has the last word.

GROUP DISCUSSION. When you hear references to the kingdom of God (for example, in the Lord's Prayer), what comes to your mind?

PERSONAL REFLECTION. Pray the Lord's Prayer (Matthew 6:9-13) with a fresh perspective of yourself as subject of the King.

The theme of the kingdom of God runs through Luke's Gospel with forty-four references. It begins as a quiet trickle that grows into a stream and becomes a river as Jesus nears the end. Watch how that trickle becomes visible in today's study. *Read Luke 4:14-30.*

---

1. What strong words and phrases throughout the passage describe how the people were responding to Jesus?

---

2. Imagining yourself as a faithful member of the congregation, describe Jesus' physical movements as he prepares to read (vv. 16-17, 20).

How would it have felt to be present at this moment?

3. When Jesus makes his claim (v. 21), what various thoughts and emotions might have rushed over the listeners?

4. Observe the Nazarenes' swift-changing attitudes toward Jesus—from praise (v. 22) to fury (v. 28). How do you account for the change?

5. You also may know people who at first were enthusiastic about Jesus. Then something happened that changed their attitude toward him. What prejudices or rationalizations did they express?

How did (or would) you respond to them?

6. *Read Luke 4:31-44.* Having been rejected by his hometown people, Jesus now makes Capernaum his base of operations. Our text logs a twenty-four-hour day of Jesus. Describe his varied activities and locations during this twenty-four-hour period.

7. From the text, how could you answer someone who calls Jesus a workaholic?

---

8. *Read Luke 5:1-16.* List the steps through which Jesus takes Simon Peter to persuade him to leave everything and follow him.

At which step can you identify with Simon Peter and why?

---

9. The leprosy healing (vv. 12-16) appears to be Luke's example of how Jesus typically helped people. What characterizes Jesus as a people helper?

---

10. Think of your ministry to others. Which of Jesus' ministering qualities do you want to have added to or reinforced in your character?

What would nurture this quality?

Pray for humility to serve Jesus as your King.

Now or Later

Consider underlining in your Bible (or marking "KG" in the margin) each reference in Luke to the kingdom of God. Here are starters: 1:33; (4:5); 4:43; 6:20; 7:28; 8:1, 10. Watch for patterns in the progression of this theme. Keep going. It gets more and more exciting!

Luke may have placed Jesus' rejection in Nazareth at the beginning of his first year of ministry as an overview of his whole Gospel. (Mark 6:1-6 places the rejection at the beginning of the second year.) Skim through Luke's Gospel to see the same major areas—people's praise and prejudice, their rejection, attempted murder and miraculous escape.

6

Opposition to Authority

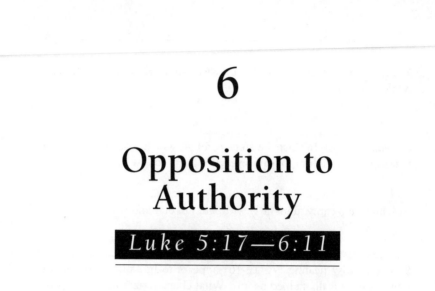

Luke 5:17—6:11

God is always full of surprises. Those who know him delight in this. But this can upset people whose security is in a system of beliefs that must be left untouched. One problem for them is that God often chooses to do something new and fresh. Then packaged religion and age-old traditions are threatened and eventually fall apart.

GROUP DISCUSSION. Has God ever surprised you? What happened?

PERSONAL REFLECTION. Perhaps God is a static vision to you—never surprising, even boring. Pray that in this study you will see God in Jesus in sometimes delightful, sometimes sobering surprises.

Jesus came on Israel's scene with astonishing teaching and activities. Two groups of religious leaders in Galilee, Pharisees and teachers of the law, mounted fierce opposition to him. They tailed him in and out of the synagogues as he ministered to people. *Read Luke 5:17—6:11,* alert to the progressive clash of authorities.

---

1. Take another look at verse 17. How does this opener help you to anticipate what's ahead?

2. Imagine yourself a part of the religious establishment, including their body language suggested in 5:17. How would Jesus' growing popularity have threatened you?

3. The six hostile encounters demonstrate the authority of Jesus. In each encounter something in his lifestyle challenges an assumption, a tradition or a prejudice. Examine below the first two assumptions that his activities challenge. What are other assumptions that he challenges?

Verses	Jesus' Radical Activities	Assumptions Jesus Challenges
5:17-26	He claimed authority to forgive sins.	*It's not possible for God to be a human being like us. Only pious people join a good religious leader, so Jesus is not such a leader.*
5:27-28	He called a tax collector to follow him.	
5:29-32	He socialized with community rejects.	
5:33-39	He led a joyous lifestyle with his disciples.	
6:1-11	He worked on the sabbath to help people.	

4. Compare the Pharisees' questions in 5:21, 30, 33 and 6:2, 7. They are implicit or explicit charges. What progression can you see from 5:21 to 6:11?

5. Jesus saw that religious legalists of his day taught a distorted view of God. What religious legalisms can keep us from enjoying the Lord and his true sabbath today?

6. What skills in answering religious critics can you learn from Jesus?

---

7. In these six episodes Jesus is exercising authority over basic areas of life (in respective order)—personal sin and guilt, relationships to fellow human beings, social life, religious lifestyle, sabbath observance. Over which area of your life do you sense a possible absence of Jesus' authority?

What is the first thing you should do to remedy this?

---

8. What do you most appreciate about Jesus in these encounters?

Thank Jesus for your fresh views of God in him and practical implications for you.

Now or Later

Sabbath observance was one of the sharpest disagreements between Jesus and the Pharisees. *Sabbath* means "to cease, to desist." See how it began, why it's important, and examples of good and bad observances: Genesis 2:2-3; Exodus 20:8-11; Isaiah 58:13; Amos 8:5.

Contemporary legalisms unfortunately still distort some people's view of God. Ask at least six people, in or out of the church, what they consider religious legalisms. Be prepared for possible strong criticisms, but don't argue with them. Be open to possibilities for opening a discussion that might help someone correct a wrong perception of God and the Bible.

7

Character of Kingdom Citizens

Luke 6:12-49

Mahatma Gandhi was India's revered leader in the fight for national independence from Britain. As a child in India, a student in England and a lawyer in South Africa, he was exposed to Christianity—and raw racism. He admired the teachings of Jesus, especially his Sermon on the Mount. He admired the life of Jesus and was inspired to follow his example. But after years of observing Christians he sadly concluded, "For me to believe in their Redeemer, their lives must show they are redeemed." He never became a Christian.

GROUP DISCUSSION. What's the difference between character and lifestyle?

PERSONAL REFLECTION. Recalling Gandhi's criticism of Christians that he observed, how well do you show that Christ has redeemed you?

Read Luke 6:12-49.

---

1. Focus on verses 12-16. The surrounding verses suggest reasons for Jesus' extended prayer time. What reasons can you find here and from your general knowledge?

2. Describe the setting and the types of people who made up the group listening to Jesus.

3. Why might the typical person on the street resist Jesus' standards?

4. To sharpen his teaching Jesus draws a contrast between the character and lifestyle of his followers and that of worldly people (vv. 24-26). What, specifically, is he warning his disciples about?

5. There are only two ways to find true happiness (blessedness)—the world's way and God's way. In what ways have you found Jesus' road the right one?

an unsatisfactory one?

6. Jesus had enemies, including his cynical brothers (John 7:2-5). He knew that loving one's enemies is impossible without strong motivation. What convictions does he say can strengthen that motivation (vv. 31-36)?

7. Jesus gives several guidelines for judging the right way. What are these guidelines (vv. 31-36)?

8. If you followed Jesus' guidelines in judging others, what positive and negative effects might it have on your relationships?

9. God is ultimately interested in how our characters are being molded. How do the illustrations about the tree and the builders reflect this?

Which one do you find more helpful? In what ways?

10. Jesus' high standards for his kingdom citizens grate against our me-first human nature. How can this passage give you hope that you can maintain his standards?

Pray for the strength you need to grow in the character and lifestyle of a kingdom citizen.

Now or Later

If an enemy is one who opposes you, who tries to frustrate your aims, Jesus had plenty of enemies! So he never asks us to do something hard that he himself did not do. Learn from his example. See Matthew 16:21-23 (Simon Peter); Luke 7:36-50 (Simon the Pharisee); 23:32-34 (those who crucified him). What gave Jesus strength to love them?

In Luke 6:27-28 Jesus gives concrete ways to love your enemy. Write down the name of your enemy, something good that you will do for them, some concrete way of blessing them and your prayer for them.

8

Five Kinds of Faith

Luke 7

An artist friend struggled over the exclusive claims of the Christian faith. In her first Bible studies she discovered an attractive Jesus. But is he the only way to God? Living in a pluralistic society had conditioned her to resist such a narrow view. Because she was still interested, some Christians pressured her to accept Jesus as her Savior and Lord. She could not.

But she privately pursued in reading the Gospels. She began to observe how differently people approached Jesus and how personally he treated each. Gradually she saw a distinction: there is indeed only one way to God—through Jesus Christ, but there are many ways to Jesus Christ.

GROUP DISCUSSION. For you, what is faith?

PERSONAL REFLECTION. What's your view of God when you approach him? powerful but remote? loving but limited? fatherly in a sentimental way? fatherly like Jesus?

In this passage we meet five persons with diverse backgrounds and varying approaches to Jesus—each expressing personal faith in a different way. Read *Luke 7*.

---

1. Describe the five individuals who met Jesus. How are their backgrounds different?

2. Focus on the first person to meet Jesus (vv. 1-10). Only twice do the Gospels record that Jesus was stirred by amazement (v. 9, and in Mark 6:6—for the opposite reason). What evidence does he have of the centurion's extraordinary faith?

3. Picture the two processions meeting just outside the city gate (vv. 11-13). There is no request for help, no outward sign of faith from the widow. (Quite different from the centurion!) What do you learn about Jesus from how he responds to the widow (vv. 13-15)?

4. It was physically easy for Jesus to touch the coffin. But by Old Testament laws he became ritualistically unclean. What comparable risks might we have to take to help a needy person?

5. Reflect on Jesus' response to John's doubt (vv. 21-23). How does it reveal his sympathy for John's spiritual crisis?

6. Jesus grabs the opportunity to teach (vv. 24-28). What is the response of his listeners (vv. 29-30)?

7. Pharisees and law experts in Jesus' audience have all the evidence but still refuse to acknowledge that both John's and Jesus' ministries are from God (vv. 29-35). How can such educated people be so intellectually dishonest?

8. One Pharisee is cautiously open. How does Jesus carefully draw out his faith (vv. 39-47)?

9. Now look back at how Jesus has communicated with the woman and with Simon. What distinctions do you notice?

What does this difference say about his understanding of each?

10. The centurion had amazing faith. The widow had passive or implicit faith. What adjective could you use to describe John's faith?

the woman's?

Simon's?

11. Of the five people, whose faith is yours most like, and how does that person challenge your faith in Jesus as teacher and Lord?

Pray for the Holy Spirit's help to take that first step in fresh obedience.

Now or Later

Faith is not some kind of religious formula to follow mechanically. Faith is active confidence in the living God; we act on what he says. *Lord* means the sovereign God who is constantly acting on our behalf. Reflect on Hebrews 11, a roll call of men and women with active confidence in the Lord. They were individuals with different challenges. But what do they have in common?

What nurtured their faith?

Give yourself a faith challenge. Take one of God's commands that you have been avoiding and obey it. For instance, "Love your enemies" or "Judge your enemy with fairness and generosity" or whatever commandment is on your conscience. Work at it! You'll find out how much practical faith you have.

9

Hearing God:
First Step of Faith

Luke 8:1-21

When the Berlin Wall cracked open, and communism began to crumble all over Eastern Europe, we rejoiced. We saw evangelistic opportunities. We heard of "tremendous openness," "thousands accepting Christ," "demand for Bibles." This was true to a certain extent. Then news articles began reporting rampant materialism and power struggles among some national church leaders. They spoke cynically of many who joined meetings simply to make western contacts.

GROUP DISCUSSION. What one or two factors most influenced your initial response to Christianity?

PERSONAL REFLECTION. Do you hear God more clearly now than at the beginning of your life with him? What has helped you to hear him better?

Wherever the Christian gospel is preached, results vary, because people have different motives for being in the audience. Jesus' knew this, and one day he dealt with this issue in a graphic way. *Read Luke 8:1-21.*

1. Luke tells us about Jesus' radical departure from tradition: women are beginning to travel with his band of disciples. What are your observations about these women (vv. 2-3)?

2. Reread the conclusion of each section in this passage (vv. 8, 15, 18, 21). What lesson is Jesus stressing in his repetition?

---

3. In the first parable (vv. 4-15) the scattered seeds are the same, but the results vary. Describe the different results.

Which of the four soils most nearly describes you?

THORNS

---

4. In contrast to the first three soils, Jesus says little about the fourth soil. He simply says it was good. But you don't need to be an expert gardener to know what makes plants grow to maturity. What is necessary?

How do these physical needs reflect spiritual needs?

---

5. Reread verse 15. What in it most helps you to retain God's message and persevere?

---

6. Jesus' second parable expands the first parable with a promise and a warning (vv. 16-18). How can Jesus' promise and warning in verse 18 motivate you to listen carefully to his teachings?

When do you tend to ignore what you know to be true from Scripture?

7. In verses 19-21 Jesus takes the opportunity to make a further point about hearing God's Word. Why does Jesus respond as he does in verse 21?

8. Home is not the easiest place to put God's Word into practice, as Jesus well knew. Describe an experience (positive or negative) you've had in putting God's Word into practice at home.

9. Reflect again on verse 15. What can you do to cultivate your good soil?

Pray for one another to be clearer witnesses to Jesus as Lord in your home.

Now or Later

If you haven't kept a journal, now is a good time to start. After you have read God's Word, experienced something significant or had a meaningful meeting with someone, reflect on what happened. Write down what you hear God saying to you. He's waiting for some intimate conversation.

James (Jesus' pragmatic brother who was converted after the resurrection) had some down-to-earth things to say about listening and doing. Compare Luke 8:21 with James 1:19-27. You can also find fruitful meditation in Psalm 119. Its 176 verses use different terms for God's Word, show various ways to approach God's Word and promise results of hearing and practicing God's Word. Try six verses a day. In a month you will cover this magnificent psalm.

10

Jesus' True Identity: Bedrock of Faith

Luke 8:22-56

At Christmas and Easter national magazines often come out with covers and feature articles like "Who Really Is Jesus?" "Can We Know the Jesus of History?" Every year new books come out like *The Jesus I Never Knew* by Philip Yancey or *Will the Real Jesus Please Stand Up?* by John Blanchard. *The Unknown Jesus* is a TV documentary series. After two thousand years the man who turned history around is still relatively unknown to most people.

GROUP DISCUSSION. What first attracted you to Jesus?

PERSONAL REFLECTION. What do you appreciate most about the person of Jesus?

When Jesus was on earth people were also puzzled about him. They also asked, "Who is this Jesus of Nazareth after all?" Luke 8 includes four power events in which Jesus reveals his real identity to the Twelve. *Read Luke 8:22-56.*

1. How do you perceive the disciples' emotions evolving from the beginning to the end of the event in verses 22-25?

2. The disciples' question at the end is one of the most important they ever ask (v. 25). They realize that they do not know Jesus as well as they thought. When have you found yourself unexpectedly becoming curious about Jesus? What did it lead to?

---

3. Describe the events in the second encounter (vv. 26-33).

---

4. Jesus delivered the man, yet the townspeople ask him to leave their region (v. 37). What might be their reasons?

---

5. In verses 40-56 Jesus and his disciples are back in home territory. The third and fourth astonishing events are intertwined. Focusing on the woman first (vv. 42-48), to your knowledge how is her healing different from other healings Jesus did?

---

6. What might be Jesus' reason(s) for his insistence on knowing who touched him?

---

7. The last power event is stretched-out agony for Jairus. Suppose you're Jairus, describing your experience with Jesus (vv. 40-56). How would you describe what you thought and felt about Jesus from the beach to the house?

8. Different people witness one or another of these four power events. Only the disciples witness all of them (only three of them at the last event). Summarize what new things they learned about Jesus during this time.

---

9. The four crisis situations were quite different from one another. Yet what similarities do you see?

---

10. What quality of Jesus here (besides love) encourages you to trust him totally in times of crisis?

Bring your nagging problems to Jesus your Lord.

Now or Later

In your journal describe to the Lord a crisis you're facing. Then be quiet and listen to him. Write out what he is saying to you. Put into practice the first step he tells you to take.

Does your church or fellowship group tend to have half-baked or stereotyped views of Jesus? What about nonchurch friends who indicate some kind of openness? You can use these power events to introduce Jesus to them. You can also use Jesus' encounters with the centurion, the widow, John the Baptist, the Pharisee and the outcast woman in Luke 7. Work out a four-to-six-week schedule for open Bible studies in homes or offices.

11

Disciple Training:
Stretched in Faith

Luke 9:1-50

"It has been my experience that superior people are attracted only by challenge. By setting our standards low and making our life soft we have quite automatically and unconsciously assured ourselves of mediocre people" (Ambassador MacWhite in *The Ugly American*, articulating his criticisms about the diplomatic corps).

GROUP DISCUSSION. How did you find yourself reacting to the ambassador's observation about superior and mediocre people?

PERSONAL REFLECTION. Do you consider yourself a mediocre or growing follower of Jesus? What evidence do you see in your life of this?

When we first look at Jesus' diplomatic corps of the Twelve, we might also question his criteria! The Gospels tell us little about their backgrounds, but they tell us much about how he trained them. *Read Luke 9:1-43.*

1. For two years Jesus has been teaching, training and testing the Twelve. Drawing on the previous chapters, in what ways has he prepared them by his example?

2. Check Jesus' commission and instructions to the Twelve. Which do you think are especially relevant for evangelism and world missions today? Why?

Which seem irrelevant or impractical? Why?

3. In verses 10-17 the apostles have just returned from their successful evangelistic mission. We can understand their reluctance to feed the hungry crowd. But Jesus persists. Observe his progressive steps to involve them in feeding the people. What are these steps?

4. Jesus now offers two hard teachings—the first prediction of his humiliating death (vv. 21-22) and the cost of commitment to him as Lord (vv. 23-27). But what long-term benefits does he promise for these short-term costs?

5. In daily life we can see this short-term costs/long-term benefits principle at work. Can you give an example?

6. What might Jesus' transfiguration have meant to the disciples?

How is Jesus' transfiguration also important for Jesus himself?

---

7. Back on the plain Jesus confronts another disciple problem. How can he be both impatient (v. 41) and compassionate at the same time (vv. 42-43)?

Think of a time when you, too, reacted with God's compassion and impatience at the same time. What did these mixed feelings cause you to do?

---

8. *Read Luke 9:43-50*, which highlights three of the disciples' problems (vv. 44-45, 46-48 and 49-50). Describe each.

What do you see as the root of these three problems?

---

9. What blind spot, or area of spiritual immaturity, do you need to work on?

---

10. Jesus is training these Twelve to carry on his world mission. What aspect of this training would benefit you?

Pray for willingness to undergo tougher discipleship training than you have had so far.

Now or Later

If your church does not yet have a defined leadership-training programme, consider starting one. Find out what other churches are effectively doing. Christian bookstores have many books on the subject. Meanwhile, begin with 1 and 2 Timothy, where Paul instructs his junior partner, Timothy, how to carry on after he (Paul) dies. Consider especially the qualifications for leaders in 1 Timothy 3:1-13.

12

God Asks Too Much

Luke 9:51—10:24

"I thought all my problems would be solved when I became a Christian. But they have increased!"

"The evangelist promised all light and joy. He said nothing about the high cost of following Jesus."

Have you heard converts say those kinds of things?

Cost? Pain? Suffering? These elements don't fit with our desire to avoid discomfort and inconvenience. Instant gratification is the order of the day for those born in the age of entitlement. No goal could be further from Jesus' way of life for his disciples.

GROUP DISCUSSION. What has been costly for you in following Jesus so far?

PERSONAL REFLECTION. God's goal for those who have chosen his way of life is to be like Jesus (Romans 8:29). Compared to pre-Christian days, how have you become more like Jesus in character?

Jesus' final yearlong journey to Jerusalem begins with an attempt to evangelize Samaritans, a people who are despised by the Jews. *Read Luke 9:51-62.*

---

1. Describe Jesus' behaviour and demeanor throughout 9:51-56.

2. Reflecting on the brief episode in 9:51-56, what can we learn about evangelism according to Jesus?

Which of these guidelines for evangelism do we as a church need to work on and why?

3. In 9:57-62 we meet three would-be disciples. What preconditions has each set for following Jesus?

Which of these three candidates for discipleship are you possibly like? In what ways?

4. *Read Luke 10:1-24.* Compare and contrast the mission of the seventy-two with the mission of the Twelve in 9:1-6.

5. Each of Jesus' instructions reveals his deep sense of urgency (10:2-12). Is it necessary for Christians today to have this kind of urgency for mission and evangelism? Why or why not?

6. For Jesus the success of the seventy-two is a preview of the ultimate overthrow of Satan (10:18). But consider his words in 10:20. How would you have felt if you were hearing this as one of the disciples?

What seems to be his aim with this caution?

---

7. Jesus expresses his elation, first to his Father and then to the seventy-two disciples. Which of his several reasons for elation move you (vv. 21-24)?

What understanding have you gained into the heart of Jesus by listening to him here?

---

8. Probably we all at one time or another have felt that God asks too much of us in discipleship and world mission. His demands are indeed serious (9:57-62; 10:1-12). But he joins them with positive appeals—explicit and implicit (9:60, 62; 10:2, 16, 18-24). Which of these appeals inspires you to pursue discipleship and world mission on his terms?

Pray for courage and spiritual energy to pursue God's goals for you.

Now or Later

The Old Testament uses the word *disciple* only once—in Isaiah 8:16. But it describes active disciples, people who committed themselves to God and his purposes and kept learning directly from him. Hebrews 11 describes some of the more prominent ones. We referred to them in the "Now or Later" question in study eight. Look at them again for lessons in discipleship training. What repeated characteristics appear in these men and women as they follow their God? What made them tough disciples? What were their rewards?

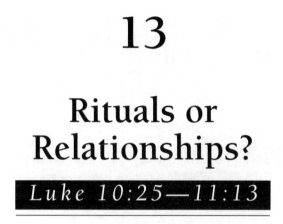

13

Rituals or Relationships?

Luke 10:25—11:13

Once in a while the media reports that a singer or actor or otherwise well-known person has converted to Christianity. Born again! We all feel good. Then a year or so later the media reports that they have been deconverted. It's not easy to tell who's a "real Christian" or an "opportunistic Christian." We know people who live by inherited Christian values and even show the Spirit's fruit. But they claim no personal relationship with God. On the other hand, some claim such a relationship with God but show no spiritual fruit.

GROUP DISCUSSION. Why do you think some people prefer a religion that has many rituals?

PERSONAL REFLECTION. Which religious rituals have helped you in the past? Which have become meaningless?

Many who physically followed Jesus were not clear about true discipleship, so Jesus keeps showing in many creative ways what qualifies a person to belong to his kingdom. *Read Luke 10:25-37.*

---

1. The man who engaged Jesus in a rabbinic debate "stood up," indicating he had been sitting with others listening to Jesus. What other facts about him can you find in 10:25-29?

2. This expert in the law knew the Old Testament rituals better than most people. But what does Jesus perceive about his knowledge of the law—the Old Testament Scripture (10:25-28)?

3. Jesus details the many concrete ways that the Samaritan "took pity" on the victim (10:33-35). What do you think he wants the expert to see?

4. Note that in 10:36 Jesus reverses the expert's original question in 10:29. The man got the point, at least intellectually, that maintaining the right relationship with God is not simply performing rituals. According to Jesus' parable, how does one demonstrate a right relationship with God?

5. In what concrete ways have you been demonstrating your relationship to God?

6. *Read Luke 10:38-42.* What positive and negative qualities do you see in Martha?

From Jesus' comment and your observation of her, what seems to be her root problem?

7. Suppose you asked Jesus, "How can I learn, like Mary, to choose what is better?" What might he say?

8. *Read Luke 11:1-13.* In the Lord's Prayer in 11:2-4, Jesus is not giving us precise words to recite. Rather, he is giving prayer topics. Sentence by sentence, what are these prayer topics?

9. Through two pictures with commentaries Jesus strongly urges us to pray with boldness. What image of God does Jesus draw in the first picture (11:5-10)?

in the second picture (11:11-13)?

10. In what ways do you need these images of Jesus to transform your prayer?

Picture God as a totally generous and always-ready friend. Then picture him as a wise and thoughtful father. Now ask him boldly for what you have not dared to ask before.

Now or Later

Think of the rituals of baptism, Holy Communion, weddings, ministerial ordinations, funerals, dedications of buildings and so on. Any customary order of worship is also a ritual. The Old Testament prescribed many rituals. Jesus participated in Jewish rituals. When do rituals help us to connect with God?

When do they get in the way of our relationship with God?

Try this prayer exercise in a group: Go through the Lord's Prayer phrase by phrase. (Use the version in Matthew 6:9-13 with its added ending.) The leader prays "Our Father," then gives time for personal reflection on that phrase and brief, verbalized responses to God. When the leader senses the appropriate time, he or she moves on to "Who art in heaven" and so on.

14

No, Not That Jesus

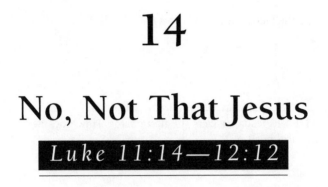

Luke 11:14—12:12

When I think of controversialists, Al comes to mind. He was one of the most effective missionaries I have known. He cheerfully provoked disagreements with almost everyone around him—his board, his colleagues, embassy clerks. His mission society didn't know what to do with him, nor what to do without him. A mutual friend confided that he was embarrassing as a fellow missionary. She would mutter and sputter, "He's too controversial." But national church leaders loved him. Those he evangelized liked him and responded to God.

GROUP DISCUSSION. How do you respond to controversies? Why?

PERSONAL REFLECTION. When have you failed to stand up for the truth about your Christian faith?

Jesus was a controversialist with the most highly trained Bible scholars of his day. He did it not for ego but because he loved the truth and hated falsehood. Jesus a passionate controversialist? No, not that Jesus. Jesus as a gentle shepherd is more manageable. But these two concepts of Jesus are necessarily complementary. *Read Luke 11:14-54.*

1. What would it have been like to be part of the crowd watching Jesus in 11:14-16? Describe what you would have seen and heard.

What are the tactics of Jesus' critics (11:15-16)?

---

2. In 11:17-20 Jesus answers the first charge. How does he point out their illogical position?

---

3. Jesus makes several stupendous claims about himself and his work (11:21-22, 23, 24-26, 27-28). How does each claim strengthen or clarify his argument?

---

4. In 11:29-36 Jesus answers his critics' second attack. His listeners knew well Jonah and Solomon in their Scriptures. In what way is Jesus comparing himself first to Jonah?

to Solomon?

---

5. Jesus ends this controversy by warning his critics that they are responsible for receiving the light (himself) right in their midst

(11:33, 36; see also 8:16-18). In what ways could we also be looking at God's light and rejecting it?

---

6. In 11:38 the Pharisee hosting a dinner party is surprised that Jesus has not ritually washed his hands after apparent contact with public uncleanness. He believes this is a "rude" response on Jesus' part. How does Jesus respond?

What religious traditions do we follow without thinking?

---

7. *Read Luke 12:1-12.* Jesus must now prepare his disciples for later persecution by these same authorities. First, he deals with the fear of powerful men. How does he distinguish between the wrong kind of fear and the proper kind of fear (12:4-7)?

---

8. Second, he promises them the help of the Holy Spirit (12:11-12). Have you had an experience similar to the one described in 12:11-12? What happened?

9. Few of us will ever engage in public religious controversy like Jesus. But there are occasions when we should stand against lies and speak the truth. What are your opportunities to do this?

In what ways is it difficult for you?

Pray for preparation and courage to be like Jesus in standing up clearly for truth.

Now or Later

Review Jesus' six woes regarding his critics in Luke 11:42-52. In three columns list (1) the six common practices of the Pharisees and experts in the law, (2) the hypocrisy behind each practice and (3) a possible parallel in modern Christian practice.

The meaning of *Satan* is "adversary." He is also called the devil ("accuser, slanderer"). In Luke 11:15 he is identified as Beelzebub (literally "lord of flies"), a Canaanite god. The Old Testament has few references to Satan: 1 Chronicles 21:1; Zechariah 3:1-2; Job 1—2. The New Testament has more references to (1) his specific activities against God's people and purposes in Mark 1:13; 4:15; Luke 13:18; 22:3, 31; Acts 5:3; 1 Corinthians 7:5; 2 Corinthians 11:14; 12:7; 1 Thessalonians 2:18; 1 Peter 5:8; Revelation 12:9; (2) God's provisions to resist Satan in Luke 4:1-13; 22:31-32; 1 Corinthians 10:12-13; Ephesians 6:11-18; James 4:7; 1 Peter 5:9; and (3) God's defeat of Satan in Luke 10:18; Romans 16:20; 1 John 3:8; Revelation 20:1-10.

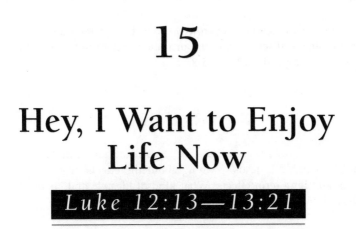

15

Hey, I Want to Enjoy Life Now

Luke 12:13—13:21

A successful stockbroker on Wall Street began a magazine article with "Greed makes the world go 'round." He used illustrations of his experiences of aggressive and risk-taking ventures in the stock market that brought millions. He claimed that the present economy is great because "honest greed" inspires people to work hard. "When we make our millions, everybody benefits. That's good old-fashioned trickle-down economy."

GROUP DISCUSSION. What's the difference between greed and desire for security?

PERSONAL REFLECTION. What might be signs in your life that material security is more important to you than trust in your Father in heaven?

Our study begins with a man who also had "honest greed." Then Jesus follows with strong warnings about God's day of judgment for those who still insist on their own lifestyle to the end, and strong appeals to repent while there's still time. *Read Luke 12:13-34.*

---

1. The man in the crowd who raised the issue was evidently a younger brother. By law his older brother would get the lion's share of the family inheritance. But economic justice was not the man's goal. Jesus' response (addressed to the crowd) shows his perception of the man's real problem. If Jesus came to our society, what might he include in "all kinds of greed" (12:14-15)?

---

2. The parable is Jesus' warning about the effects of greed—short-term and long-term effects. What kind of lifestyle and character has the rich man developed?

---

3. This man is called "the rich fool." But you and I probably also know poor fools and middle-class fools. According to Jesus' parable, what makes a person a fool?

---

4. In 12:22-34 we find the answer to greed: trusting in God. What does worrying suggest about our concept of God?

---

5. *Read Luke 12:35-59.* In the first parable, Jesus pictures that relationship as servants' total loyalty to their master (12:35-40), whether or not he is physically present. If you believed that Jesus would physically return next week, how would that affect your agenda for the next few days?

6. In the second parable how are leaders to prove their loyalty to Jesus (12:41-48)?

7. In 12:49-53 Jesus points to one sign of the coming crisis of God's judgment. Describe what is taking place here.

8. Jesus urges his listeners to interpret correctly current signs of his soon return—his very presence, then his teachings and his works (12:54-56). Finally, Jesus describes "you" on the way to court for debts (12:57-59). How is the last scene the application of the first two scenes?

9. *Read Luke 13:1-9.* Jesus is speaking to the assumption that people who die violently must have been terrible sinners. Why is it easier to judge others' sinfulness than to check our own spiritual condition?

10. In the parable of the fruitless fig tree, Jesus is picturing Israel and her need for national repentance. To what extent could this parable also apply to our nation?

11. List your past week's activities and personal concerns. Which values and goals do they reflect—those of God's kingdom or those of this world?

Pray to know how to bring about needed changes in your church in the area of materialism.

Now or Later

12. *Read Luke 13:10-17,* the last time we see Jesus teaching in a synagogue. This sabbath conflict summarizes the contrast between Israel's religion and God's kingdom. You can see this contrast in how differently the ruler and Jesus viewed the woman (vv. 14-16). What's the difference?

13. *Read Luke 13:18-21.*What do these mini-parables add to your understanding of the kingdom of God?

Maybe Jesus knew this old Jewish saying: "If we keep more than we need, we're stealing from the poor." Rework your finances so you can give more money to charitable organizations that you believe in but have never supported. If you do this with Jesus as your financial consultant, things will change! You will enjoy life in positive ways.

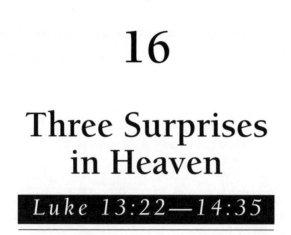

16

Three Surprises in Heaven

Luke 13:22—14:35

A prediction making the rounds these days is quite instructive. When you get to heaven, you're going to have three surprises. First, you'll be surprised who will not be there. Second, you'll be surprised who will be there. Third, you'll be surprised that you are there!

What a gentle way to keep us humble: not to be sure we have the last word about who will pass through the pearly gates and who will not. It should lead us to think again about God's grace.

GROUP DISCUSSION. Before you became a Christian, what was your biggest question about salvation?

PERSONAL REFLECTION. Think of how Jesus' salvation has been transforming you. Thank and praise him for specific changes.

The question about assurance of salvation is important to ask. People asked Jesus about this in different ways: "What must I do to inherit eternal life?" "How can a man be born again when he is old?" "Who then can be saved?" In today's text they ask, "Lord, are only a few people going to be saved?" *Read Luke 13:22-35.*

1. It was commonly believed that Israel would be saved and that God was preparing the messianic feast for Israel. What facts in Jesus' para-

ble and commentary would have shocked his nationalistic listeners (13:24-30)?

How do you respond emotionally and intellectually to 13:24-27?

2. Based on this parable, how would you answer a skeptic who thinks God's conditions for salvation are too narrow (13:24)?

3. Bible scholar Craig Keener calls 13:31-35 "Lament of the Rejected Lover." In what ways do you think this title is valid?

4. *Read Luke 14:1-24.* What reasons could you suggest for the Pharisees' repeated silence in response to Jesus' questions (14:4, 6)?

5. Jesus teaches the guests what true honor is (14:7-11), and he teaches his host what true hospitality is (14:12-14). In each case, what human weakness has he put his finger on?

---

6. Suppose a seeker asks you, "What kinds of people qualify for heaven?" You could use Jesus' parable in 14:15-24 to answer him or her. How could you summarize it in two or three sentences?

---

7. *Read Luke 14:25-35.* Jesus takes the opportunity to spell out his condition for discipleship: total loyalty to him. He challenges two powerful loyalties—to family and to self. What might be an example of Christians "hating" their families?

"hating" themselves?

---

8. What does it mean for Christians to carry their cross of execution (14:27)?

---

9. Jesus never sweet-talks anyone into following him. He makes it clear that following him has a high price tag. The two mini-parables seem to make the same point about this (14:28-33). But in the second parable, what twist does he give to the same challenge?

10. For you, what would be the cost of not following Jesus on his terms?

Confess to the Lord the shortcomings he has been showing you. Receive his grace for forgiveness and a new start.

Now or Later

When Jesus says we should hate our parents, he is using a hyperbole (an intended exaggeration not to be taken literally). In his Jewish culture (as in many non-Western cultures), obedience to parents was absolute. So the total commitment he asks of followers cuts right across this cultural norm. Our love and loyalty to Jesus as Lord must be uncompromising.

When our parents demand an obedience that clashes with loyalty to Jesus, and we have to say no to them, it appears that we hate them (see Luke 12:49-53). Jesus himself had to make that hard choice of who was first in his life. See (in chronological order) Luke 2:48-50; John 2:3-5; Mark 3:31-35. See also evidence of his obeying the fifth commandment of honouring parents in Luke 2:51 and John 19:25-27.

17

Parable of Two Lost Sons

Luke 15

The title of Rembrandt's famous painting *The Return of the Prodigal Son* focuses on the father's younger son in Jesus' well-known parable. But by composition and lighting, the artist causes us rightfully to focus on the father—his face lined by longsuffering, his body bent toward his kneeling son, his hands gently embracing his ragged boy.

Some evangelists stress the sins and repentance of the young man so much that the father's compassion and celebration fade away. His repentance is important. But in Jesus' parable it is the suffering, then rejoicing father who dominates the picture.

GROUP DISCUSSION. When did you first see the joyful side of God's nature?

PERSONAL REFLECTION. Religious leaders strongly criticized Jesus for going to parties and apparently enjoying the social outcasts there. Try visualizing Jesus enjoying you and your friends.

In this section of Luke Jesus presents three stories as one parable. *Read Luke 15.*

1. Describe the context for these parables from verses 1-2.

2. All three parables have the theme of an owner losing something valuable and then throwing a party when it is found. Jesus uses the two brief stories to lead up to the climactic third story. In broad strokes how is this third story different?

3. Focus on verses 11-13. The younger son's opening words and subsequent action reveal his attitude toward his father. What do you perceive?

4. In verses 13-16 Jesus summarizes the younger son's experience "in a far country." What is your attitude toward the son as you read these verses and why?

5. From the young man's plans in verses 17-19 would you say he is in repentance. Why or why not?

How did your repentance begin, and how did it progress from there?

6. Visualize the father's actions as his son (probably) waits at the town gate (vv. 20-24). In light of verse 2, what does Jesus want his critics to see about this father (Jesus himself)?

7. In the father's interaction with the older son, what other dimensions of the father's character and motives are revealed (vv. 28-32)?

8. Jesus intends the younger son to portray the tax collectors and "sinners" (v. 1). He has painted a negative portrait of the elder son, who represents the Pharisees and teachers of the law (v. 2). Where in his parable can you see Jesus extending hope to his critics (vv. 28-32)?

9. The rejoicing nature of God was foreign, if not downright offensive, to Jesus' critics. The same is true of contemporary "Pharisees." What may be reasons for their discomfort with a God who likes to throw parties?

10. No matter how prodigal he was, the younger son knew his identity—he was his father's son (vv. 12, 17-21). On the other hand, the elder son never expresses this relationship. He sees the old man as an unfair slave driver (v. 29). In what ways do you find yourself in tension between these two views of God?

Ask God to open your eyes to see him as the father in this study.

Now or Later

Old Testament believers never addressed God as Father, though once in a while a writer says that God is like a father (Psalm 103:13). It was Jesus who first taught his followers to approach and address God as Father. Remember Luke 11:2-13? Go through the Gospel of Luke and highlight all the verses where Jesus refers to God as Father. In what ways should these fatherly portraits influence your relationship to God?

Instead of waiting for the prodigals to come to church (they won't), go out to where they are in that "far country." In any good-sized town there are increasingly more shelters for the homeless and the domestically abused, rehabilitation centers for drug abusers, halfway houses for former prison inmates. You might find a ministry to prostitutes or runaway teenagers. Call and find out what your church can do to befriend these lonely individuals.

18

Parables on
Smart Money

At the dinner table someone mentioned the newspaper article reporting that one percent of Americans own forty percent of the nation's resources. Then we talked about how inordinately rich some families are. Out of sight for mere mortals like us! My nephew said quite firmly, "Inherited money is not respected." Then he added wistfully, "But I sure wish I had some."

GROUP DISCUSSION. What do you like about money?

PERSONAL REFLECTION. What recent experience may be a clue that your attitude to money needs changing?

We have mixed feelings and opinions about money; Jesus did not. We saw that in Luke 12. He never condemned riches, only their misuse. Jesus' two parables here tell us where the smart money is. *Read Luke 16.*

1. How do you respond to the actions of the manager in this story (vv. 1-7)?

2. Jesus' parable is quite straightforward. His application, however,

doesn't seem as clear (vv. 8-9). How does he seem to be applying the parable to his disciples?

3. Greed and dishonesty often go together, and in verses 10-15 Jesus clearly condemns both of these traits. How is Jesus defining dishonesty?

4. Look again at verses 8-12. What principles of money management can you draw from this passage?

5. Consider the sharp words that Jesus has for the Pharisees (vv. 13-18). What do they add to his teaching about the use of money?

6. In verses 19-22 Jesus contrasts the earthly status of the rich man and of Lazarus. What impresses you most about the differences?

7. Then Jesus spends the rest of his parable contrasting their different eternal status. The rich man is a dramatic example of what happens when one uses God's possessions wrongly. How did he use God's resources dishonestly in this life (vv. 19-21)?

---

8. Verses 23-26 give us the most graphic picture of heaven and hell in the Bible. What facts—open and hidden—do you observe about these dimensions of existence?

---

9. In the last part of his dialogue with Abraham we can learn more about life on the other side of eternity. What especially do you learn about the relationship of Scripture ("Moses and the Prophets") and eternal salvation (vv. 27-31)?

---

10. Our relatives and friends are probably not all skeptics like the man's brothers. Let Jesus' revelation of life after death spur us on to witness to our loved ones. What more can you do to tell them about Jesus' way of life before it's too late?

Help each other pray for the salvation of people you love.

Now or Later

We sometimes see valid offers of a good investment, and we think how good it would be to earn more money to give away. But the financial institution requires a greater layout than we as individuals have. Try what some have done for the kingdom of God: pool your individually limited resources. Join others to get that certificate of deposit or whatever pays good interest. You'll all grow spiritually richer!

19

Pictures of Hanging In There

Luke 17:1—18:14

Reports and photos of survivors in horrendous disasters fascinate us. There's Elian, the six-year-old Cuban boy who clung to an inner tube for two days off the Florida coast while his mother and others drowned trying to escape from Cuba. There's that fifty-year-old woman in Taiwan pulled out alive from a twelve-story building eight days after it was demolished by an earthquake. And there's that family in Siberia still devoted to Jesus Christ after years of communist persecution.

GROUP DISCUSSION. When has it been the hardest for you to persevere as a Christian?

PERSONAL REFLECTION. How willing are you to admit failures, get up and keep going with the Lord?

Jesus knew firsthand about hanging in there. He had to persevere in his goals in the face of family misunderstanding, brutal opposition and temptation to take the easy way. *Read Luke 17:1-19.*

---

1. Why do the disciples respond so strongly to Jesus in 17:5?

2. Jesus responds with two pictures (17:6, 7-10). In what way does each picture tell the disciples how faith increases?

3. The Samaritan alone returns to Jesus. How does his action demonstrate "increasing" faith?

4. *Read Luke 17:20-37*. The Pharisees expected the kingdom of God to be visible and earthly—in other words, the political state of Israel freed from Roman rule. How does Jesus' teaching on the kingdom of God clash with their idea (17:20-21)?

5. Jesus warns them not to be misled by false prophets (17:22-23). What modern prophets do you think are misleading people?

6. What does Jesus' metaphor of lightning warn about the nature of his coming (17:24)?

7. Citing two Old Testament examples, Jesus warns about people's lack of preparation for God's judgment. You can probably see the parallels between those generations and our generation (17:26-29). Consider the powerful influences in our culture. How can these influences mislead us?

8. *Read Luke 18:1-14.* Jesus is continuing his instructions on how to live while waiting for his return (18:1, 8): *Don't give up praying.* What are some reasons that people give up praying?

9. To encourage us to persist in praying, Jesus draws a portrait of a helpless widow stubbornly appealing to a heartless judge. But how is God different from the judge?

Perhaps our view of God is like the heartless judge. How can we correct that view?

10. On the other hand, persistence in prayer can lead to presumption about God. Jesus balances this temptation with the parable of the Pharisee and tax collector (18:9-14). From his prayer, how would you describe the Pharisee's concept of God—and himself?

What are the tax collector's views?

---

11. What do you think your prayers might reveal about your concept of God—and yourself?

Pray as honestly and as briefly as the tax collector did.

Now or Later

Those famous polls report that two-thirds of Americans say they pray at home. What would be the percentage if the question were "pray regularly with others"? Praying with others helps us to persevere together. Jesus urges us to do so (Matthew 18:19-20). Look at what happened when the early Christians persisted in praying together: Acts 1:14, 24; 2:42; 4:23-31; 6:6-7; 12:12; 13:1-3; 14:23.

If you are not yet in a prayer group, start one with one or two others. Watch it grow as you together hang in there for the kingdom of God.

20

The Nobodies God Wants in His Kingdom

Luke 18:15—19:10

We may not be aware of it but many of our churches look, feel and act quite middle-class. I once invited a former prison inmate who had been soundly converted to Christ to my church. He paid good attention to what was going on—while wriggling nonstop. I finally asked if he was okay. He muttered, "Yeah, yeah." The church members I introduced him to were even more nervous than he was. Afterward he confided, "I feel like a nobody here." He is now thriving as worship leader in a halfway-house chapel.

GROUP DISCUSSION. In your community, who is viewed as an insignificant nobody?

PERSONAL REFLECTION. In all honesty, who in your community have you secretly considered valueless?

Jesus customarily worshipped and taught in local synagogues. But he was also constantly out on the streets, in the fields, in the marketplace, available to any and all. Now in the last few weeks of his life, as he and his disciples near Jerusalem, the crowds grow bigger and hotter with messianic fever. And "nobodies" keep interrupting him along the way. *Read Luke 18:15—19:10.*

---

1. The disciples demonstrate their society's attitude toward children as insignificant while Jesus gives them eternal significance (18:16-17). He says they have characteristics that qualify people for God's kingdom. What characteristics does this include?

2. From 18:18-30 what do we know about the rich young ruler?

In what ways is Jesus' particular test in 18:22 applicable to us?

3. The disciples are astonished by Jesus' comment about the rich (18:24-26). The Old Testament thinking was that riches are a sign of God's blessing. How does Jesus answer them?

4. Jesus' fourth prediction to the Twelve about his coming death is found in 18:31-34. They still have no idea what he's talking about! How could you explain this lack of understanding?

What may be our reasons for hearing God selectively?

---

5. The second "nobody" interrupts the Jesus procession (18:35-43). Why do you think Jesus stops in his tracks?

---

6. Jesus' question of the beggar is interesting. How might you explain to a curious seeker why Jesus asked this obvious question (18:40-42)?

---

7. Focus now on 19:1-10. Jericho was a prosperous agricultural and commercial city, a popular oasis resort for royalty and priests. In such a city, what kind of character would a chief tax collector likely develop?

---

8. What other side of Zacchaeus comes to the surface in 19:3-6 and 8?

9. Some scholars see this Zacchaeus story as a mini-gospel. What main points of the Christian gospel can you discern in it?

10. In these encounters with Jesus, Luke has carefully recorded people's reactions to three "nobodies" and one "somebody" (18:15, 26, 39; 19:7). What lesson is he giving us?

Confess your sins of ignoring the nobodies in your community or church and ask God to show you how to reach out.

Now or Later

Think of the outsiders or nobodies in the community that you are at least remotely acquainted with. Considering Jesus' example, discuss concretely what your church can do to reach out to them.

In our churches we tend to be impressed with the professional people, the influential business executives, the community leaders—the so-called movers and shakers—while others feel insignificant. They come and go as though they are invisible. Program some regular creative activities that could include the invisible people comfortably.

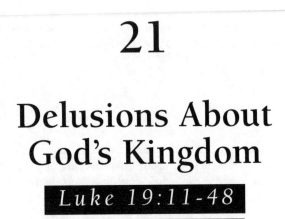

21

Delusions About God's Kingdom

Luke 19:11-48

All my bosses have been hard drivers who regularly exasperated me. But in the long run we worked together productively because we were committed to the aims of the organization. If we respect and like our bosses, we're willing to work hard. If we don't respect them, if we're suspicious of their motives, we usually don't work hard. Then we become unproductive.

GROUP DISCUSSION. In your opinion, what makes a good boss?

PERSONAL REFLECTION. Are you having problems with your boss—or any authority figure? How would you like that situation changed?

Likewise, our personal view of God as our ultimate Boss affects our working relationship to him. And productivity has eternal consequences. *Read Luke 19:11-27.*

---

1. Some key words in 19:10 have evidently inflamed the crowd's messianic expectations. Jesus' parable aims to counter any false hopes. In verses 12-15, what similarities between the nobleman and Jesus can you see?

2. The master gives each servant a mina (the equivalent of three months' wages, a quarter of your annual salary). His instruction is to "put it to work" until he returns. If you were one of the servants, what is the first thing you would do to "put it to work" for the best returns?

3. The day of reckoning has arrived, for the master has returned as king (vv. 15-26). The rewarding of the first two servants is simple. How fair or unfair do you consider the punishment for the third servant? Explain.

4. Jesus' parable teaches a principle of stewardship summarized in verse 26. Where in your experience or observation have you seen this principle at work?

5. The enemies of the nobleman-made-king are mentioned only at the beginning and here at the end (vv. 14, 27). Jesus is referring to Israel's national leaders. How, then, does his prophetic parable aim to point out their delusions about the kingdom of God?

6. *Read Luke 19:28-48*, the prelude to Jesus' last week. Then fill out the chart below.

Jesus' Activity	What Is Revealed About Jesus
He prepares to enter Jerusalem (vv. 28-36).	In control of event/details as he instructs the disciples
He approaches Jerusalem (vv. 37-40).	
He reflects on Jerusalem (41-44).	
He enters the temple area (vv. 45-46).	
He teaches at the temple (vv. 47-48).	

7. In this panoramic view of Jesus the Messiah, what do you find hard to understand about him?

8. What do you discover here about Jesus that you positively respond to? Why?

9. What changes in lifestyle and new disciplines would make you a more accountable servant?

Ask God for deeper conviction about being an accountable servant, especially in view of his coming judgment.

Now or Later

The final judgment will be the climax of history. Biblical teachings on judgment are not scare tactics, but realistic warnings about the nature of evil and justice in the universe. They urge us to be responsible and accountable to God. See Psalm 96:13; Acts 17:31; Romans 14:12; 1 Corinthians 3:10-15; 15:24-28; 2 Corinthians 5:9-10; 2 Thessalonians 1:7-9; Hebrews 9:27; Revelation 20:10.

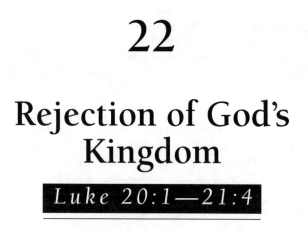

22

Rejection of God's Kingdom

Luke 20:1—21:4

I remember a situation where a humanist on campus tried to brand the Christian students as a bunch of losers. He boasted that he did not need religion for a crutch as they did. His intense hostility left me speechless. Then I thought of three perfect answers—late that night in bed.

GROUP DISCUSSION. How do you know when to defend your faith and when not to?

PERSONAL REFLECTION. Do you tend to be outspoken or mousy about your faith?

Most of us are not quick to think on our feet, and certainly not as quick and sharp as Jesus. We have seen him as a fearless controversialist in Galilee (study fourteen). Now we will see him in the capital, taking on four distinct authority groups as each hurls their theological rocks at him. *Read Luke 20:1-26.*

---

1. In 20:1-8 the leaders are right to question the authority of any popular teacher making cosmic claims. But what do you perceive about their attitude and style of debate with Jesus?

2. Typically Jesus takes the opportunity to show God's side of the story. By parable and commentary he warns of God's coming judgment on them and the Israel they represent (20:9-18). How do you find yourself responding to his stern characterization of God?

3. The same group sets a second trap. Instead, they fall into their own trap when Jesus challenges their wrong assumption about politics and religion. How does he correct that view (20:23-26)?

What has been a political-religious tension not yet resolved for you as a Christian?

4. *Read Luke 20:27-47.* To ridicule Jesus and his teaching about life after death, the Sadducees tell a hypothetical story. Jesus responds with facts about life after death that contradict their view. What are these facts (20:34-38)?

5. "Clever" people today still try to mock and explain away facts inconvenient to their humanistic system of beliefs. What examples do you know?

6. How does this teaching compare to your own view of life after death?

7. Jesus initiates the last controversy (20:41-44). What issues is he drawing out?

This is Jesus' last word to the disciples (only four days before they see him crucified). How do you think he might be feeling after all these debates?

8. Jesus moves from theological discussion to practical realities. He warns his disciples (with others eavesdropping) of the evil practices of the teachers of the law (vv. 45-47). What can cause educated religious people (anywhere) to be so close-minded?

9. All four groups reject Jesus as God's Messiah/King. After this there are no more debates on the truth—only arrest, trial and death. How can we maintain biblical truth against the enemies of Christianity today?

10. *Read Luke 21:1-4,* which Luke links with 20:47. What does this brief episode tell you about the kind of faith that Jesus values?

Picture your faith being like the widow's kind of faith. Talk to God about what you see.

Now or Later

We have been looking at Jesus as a powerful controversialist in his battle for truth. He was grounded in God's Word and its practical implications. Contemporary Christianity badly needs apologists— men and women who know how to defend their biblical faith. Find someone who can train you to stand up and speak up clearly, strongly for truth.

23

Jesus' Predictions of the Last Days

Luke 21:5-38

Biblical interpretations of the last days can stir up some people, especially when the Middle East is in the news. Others react against what they perceive as sensationalism by avoiding any consideration of biblical prophecies. Even secular magazines and newspapers are noting the proliferation of religious books on the last days. Some are worth reading. Others are not. They sell well because people want some authority to tell them what's coming in the future.

GROUP DISCUSSION. How do you usually respond to biblical texts or discussions on the last days?

PERSONAL REFLECTION. What makes you glad about the last days? What scares you?

In today's study the Lord Jesus shows us how to keep a balance by being properly informed and obedient to his instructions. *Read Luke 21:5-38.*

---

1. What are your overall impressions of Jesus' talk on the end of this age?

2. Jesus' prophecy of the destruction of Jerusalem and its temple demolishes the disciples' expectation as to how they might gain political and religious power. What ideas or expectations do you have regarding the kingdom of God?

3. Describe the kinds of troubles that will take place (vv. 8-17).

4. What does Jesus want the disciples to gain from this teaching (vv. 8, 9, 14-19)?

5. Why are some Christians more taken up with signs than with Jesus' instructions?

6. In verses 25-28 Jesus does seem to give some final signs that will occur just before he returns. How are these different from the activities in verses 10-11? (Recall also his word in 17:19.)

7. How is Jesus' parable of the fig tree (vv. 29-31) related to his preceding teachings about his return in glory?

8. Jesus teaches us how to live in view of the coming events and intensifying troubles. Gather up his counsel and warnings (vv. 8, 9, 14, 28, 29, 34-36). Which particular warning grabs you? Why?

9. Which one of his promises gives you strong incentive to be prepared for Jesus' return (vv. 14-15, 19, 24, 31, 33)?

10. Earthly preoccupations can make us insensitive to spiritual realities and therefore unprepared to "stand before the Son of Man" (vv. 5, 34-36). What earthly activity tempts you this way?

11. It has been said, "Live as though Jesus may return today. Work as though he won't return for thirty years." What practical things can we do to keep this balance?

Pray for this balance to work out in your life in practical ways.

Now or Later

The second coming of Messiah Jesus is seen prophetically in Daniel 7:13–14 as the Son of Man. In the New Testament the following aspects of his return are highlighted: suddenly and unmistakably (Matthew 24:27, 36–41); visibly, bodily (Acts 1:11); universally (Revelation 1:7); triumphantly (Philippians 2:9–11); conclusively (1 Thessalonians 4:13–17) and practically (1 Thessalonians 5:1–11). For further studies on this subject see 1 Thessalonians 4:13—5:11; 2 Thessalonians 1—3; 2 Timothy 3:1–9; 2 Peter 2—3 and the book of Revelation.

24

Jesus, Our Passover Lamb

Luke 22:1-46

We don't have sheep in Hawaii. But we know what they look like and what they're like. One Sunday in our Bible class we reflected on an enlarged photo of a lamb. He lay on his side. His feet were bound together in two pairs. People were intrigued. A few immediately knew who that represented. We meditated on this picture for a few minutes, then shared insights. It graphically introduced the concept of the sacrificial lamb.

GROUP DISCUSSION. Can you recall your most moving celebration of Holy Communion? What made it so moving?

PERSONAL REFLECTION. What was going on in your heart the last time you participated in Holy Communion?

This section of Scripture takes us into the saddest days of history. With Judas's help the nation's leaders completed their plot to kill the Son of God. But these days are also the greatest days on earth for Jesus. He has accomplished his life mission, and he confirmed to the Twelve that they will carry on his global mission. So with them he establishes his new Passover to supersede the old Passover. *Read Luke 22:1-38*.

1. What do verses 1-6 reveal about the religious leaders?

2. History shows that betrayal of a friend or even a family member is not unique. But what puts Judas's betrayal in a class by itself?

3. Compare Jesus' plans with the authorities' plans. As you examine his plans, what impresses you about Jesus himself?

4. Since his childhood Jesus had witnessed the sacrificing of the lamb in Jerusalem's temple, knowing that would some day be himself. Try to see what all this meant to him during his last intimate Passover supper with his closest friends. What do you perceive as his deepest concerns (vv. 14-23)?

5. Jesus is our new Passover Lamb (vv. 19-20)! What are the implications for you?

6. Focus on verses 24-38. When you have been faced with this kind of leadership rivalry in your group, what did you do?

7. In view of the disciples' pettiness, Jesus' next words to them are astonishing (vv. 28-30). How can he have such confidence in these immature, obtuse, self-serving men?

8. Jesus further prepares them, especially Peter, for the crisis coming in the next few hours. He has been grooming Peter to replace him as team leader. As Peter, what might you be thinking and feeling as you hear Jesus' words (vv. 31-32)?

---

9. *Read Luke 22:39-46.* What guidelines for praying can you find in Jesus' example and words?

---

10. What weaknesses and failures do you want to acknowledge as you compare yourself to the disciples?

Jesus, our new Passover Lamb, died for each of our sins. Confess them before you go out to serve him with new strength.

Now or Later

Read Exodus 11—12 for the background and detailed instructions for celebrating this well-loved feast of Israel in early spring. The symbolism of "Christ our Passover lamb" (1 Corinthians 5:7) and "Lamb of God" (John 1:29) means that Jesus' death completed and fulfilled the Jewish ritual by bringing about God's new and universal rescue of his people.

Inquire at a Jewish synagogue or messianic Jewish congregation about participating in their Passover celebration. They would welcome you. Get *God's Appointed Times* by Barney Kasdan, a highly readable guide for understanding and celebrating the biblical holidays. It includes order of service, graphics, songs, games, menus, recipes (some very good!), Scriptures, prayers and so on. Order it from Jews for Jesus, 60 Haight Street, San Francisco, CA 94102.

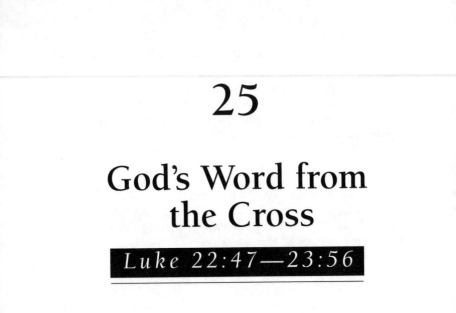

25

God's Word from the Cross

Luke 22:47—23:56

The symbol of the cross is used in many ways—on and in Christian churches, by the Red Cross, on many European flags. It is used as jewelry, even by people with no allegiance to Christ. But they would not think of wearing a burnished gold miniature of an electric chair or an injection needle around their necks. In Jesus' time the crude wooden cross meant capital punishment for the worst criminals.

Under Roman law Jesus died as a criminal. In God's eternal plan Jesus died as the sacrificial substitute for us sinners. Many hymns and gospel songs retain this core truth. (Few contemporary songs do that.) Approach this study prayerfully for a deeper understanding of the death of Jesus.

GROUP DISCUSSION. In what circumstances did you first understand the meaning of Jesus' cross?

PERSONAL REFLECTION. Has reflection on Jesus' death ever deeply moved you? Why or why not?

Read Luke 22:47-62, feeling the drama of Jesus' arrest on the Mount of Olives.

---

1. In a word or phrase, how would you describe Jesus as he relates to each individual or group during his arrest?

2. Only a few hours after Simon Peter swore unique loyalty to Jesus, he makes an about-face. In what kind of situation are you tempted to avoid identification with Jesus and his cause?

3. To have Jesus executed the Jewish council needs a political indictment of treason from the Roman governor Pilate. *Read Luke 23:1-31.* Jesus is silent, or nearly so, before Governor Pilate and King Herod (23:3, 9; see also 22:67). What reasons can you think of for his silence?

4. Three times Pilate says he finds no valid charge against Jesus and seeks to release him (23:4, 13-17, 22). Why then do you think he ultimately pronounces the death penalty?

5. *Read 23:32-56.* How do you picture the appearance of the faces of each group or individual as they watch the man on the cross?

Luke says little about Jesus' physical death. Instead he focuses on people's attitudes to the man on the centre cross. What attitude toward Jesus does each group or individual reveal?

6. Luke highlights one of the criminals, the only person with whom Jesus personally dialogues. What may be Luke's reason for this focus (23:39-43)?

7. Throughout his six hours on the cross, Jesus is in touch with his Father. What do his brief words to the Father reflect about their relationship (23:34, 46)?

8. Luke carefully records the physical phenomena occurring at the point of Jesus' last breath (23:44-45). What meaning can we gain from these events? (See also Hebrews 10:19-25.)

9. What can we as the church do to make God's word from the cross relevant to our needy world?

10. How could the cross become more central and significant to your own life?

Pray that together you and your fellow believers will make a difference in your community because you have heard God's word from the cross of Jesus.

Now or Later

The Gospels do not interpret the meaning of Jesus' death. Other parts of the Bible do so with varying emphases: (1) the substitutionary nature of his sacrificial death (Isaiah 52:13—53:12); (2) God's righteousness, not ours (Romans 3:21-26); (3) destruction of Satan's kingdom (Colossians 2:15; 1 John 3:8); (4) new relationship with God (Romans 5:8-11; 2 Corinthians 5:15-19); (5) sin's power over the broken, victory assured (Romans 6:5-11; Galatians 3:13-14; Hebrews 2:14-15; 1 John 1:7-9); (6) eternity with God guaranteed (Romans 5:6-11; 8:31-39).

Think through how to explain the good news of Jesus' death to a seeker. You can combine Luke 23:32-43 (or 23:44-49) with a gospel summary like 2 Corinthians 5:21 or 8:9, or Titus 3:4-6. Look for an opportunity to share what you are learning.

26

God's Word from the Empty Tomb

Luke 24

How could you destroy Christianity? Explain away Jesus' resurrection. For instance, you could say the highly emotional women at the tomb were deluded. Or argue they went to the wrong tomb. You might dismiss the disciples' witness by saying they had hallucinations. All else failing, you could insist that the resurrection was spiritual, not physical. From the first Easter till now the enemies of the church have tried to get rid of the historical facts (Matthew 28:11–15). None have succeeded. For how else do you explain the empty tomb?

GROUP DISCUSSION. Which do you like to celebrate more—Christmas or Easter? Why?

PERSONAL REFLECTION. How did you spend Easter? Was it special or just another holiday?

Read Luke 24.

---

1. The women who go to the tomb in verses 1-12 are a personal link between the cross and the empty tomb (23:55-56). Suppose you were one of them, excitedly telling the disciples about the empty tomb. How would you feel when the men respond with "Nonsense! You're crazy"?

2. If you were Peter dashing to the tomb (v. 12), what would you be thinking and feeling?

---

3. From verses 13-35, what kind of people do the two disciples seem to be?

---

4. What strikes you about the stranger's approach and his dialogue with them (vv. 12-27)?

---

5. In his rebuke Jesus identifies the cause of the disciples' despair—reluctance to accept the (real meaning of) Scriptures about the Messiah's suffering (v. 25). Describe the last time you were challenged to change your view about a major biblical event or teaching.

---

6. Look at 24:36-53 as a seeker sincerely examining the facts about Jesus' resurrection. Which facts or implications intrigue you?

Which puzzle you?

---

7. For three or so years Jesus has been preparing his disciples to carry on his world mission. He now climaxes this training by stressing systematic, in-depth Bible understanding (vv. 25-27, 32, 44-47). In what ways can you testify to this importance in your life and witness?

8. Verse 49 is expanded in John 14:16 and Acts 1:4-5. For evangelism we need both Bible study and the Holy Spirit. What happens when you're strong on one side and weak on the other?

9. Reflect on your studies of Jesus Christ—his life with people, his death as a criminal, his resurrection. What for you are specific incentives to be his "witness of these things"?

10. How can you take Jesus' message of new hope and new joy to your community?

Praise God with the angels for Jesus' resurrection! Pray that his new life in you and in your church would be let loose in your world.

Now or Later

Examine 1 Corinthians 15, Paul's classic apology on the universal implications of Jesus' resurrection for the very existence of the Christian church and for our personal resurrection. See also Romans 6:5-14; Philippians 3:10-11; 1 Thessalonians 4:13-17.

Jesus' resurrection cannot be separated from his commission to his followers. Every Christian should eventually be as familiar with the facts and implications of Jesus' resurrection as were the first Christians. This was the bedrock of faith for the twelve apostles in their preaching, teaching, healing and other ministries (Acts 2:24-36; 3:15-16; 4:2, 10-12, 33 and so on). This was also true for the apostle Paul (Acts 13:29-35; 17:18, 31-32; 23:6; 24:15, 21).

> Jesus' resurrection
> demonstrates he is the King of hope and joy,
> guarantees our only hope for eternal life with God,
> and urges us to be his witnesses to the world.
> What joy!

Leader's Notes

MY GRACE IS SUFFICIENT FOR YOU. (2 COR 12:9)

Leading a Bible discussion can be an enjoyable and rewarding experience. But it can also be *scary*—especially if you've never done it before. If this is your feeling, you're in good company. When God asked Moses to lead the Israelites out of Egypt, he replied, "O Lord, please send someone else to do it!" (Ex 4:13). It was the same with Solomon, Jeremiah and Timothy, but God helped these people in spite of their weaknesses, and he will help you as well.

You don't need to be an expert on the Bible or a trained teacher to lead a Bible discussion. The idea behind these inductive studies is that the leader guides group members to discover for themselves what the Bible has to say. This method of learning will allow group members to remember much more of what is said than a lecture would.

These studies are designed to be led easily. As a matter of fact, the flow of questions through the passage from observation to interpretation to application is so natural that you may feel that the studies lead themselves. This study guide is also flexible. You can use it with a variety of groups—student, professional, neighborhood or church groups. Each study takes forty-five to sixty minutes in a group setting.

There are some important facts to know about group dynamics and encouraging discussion. The suggestions listed below should enable you to effectively and enjoyably fulfil your role as leader.

Preparing for the Study

1. Ask God to help you understand and apply the passage in your own life. Unless this happens, you will not be prepared to lead others. Pray too for the various members of the group. Ask God to open your hearts to the message of his Word and motivate you to action.

2. Read the introduction to the entire guide to get an overview of the entire book and the issues which will be explored.

3. As you begin each study, read and reread the assigned Bible passage to familiarize yourself with it.

4. This study guide is based on the New International Version of the Bible. It will help you and the group if you use this translation as the basis for your study and discussion.

5. Carefully work through each question in the study. Spend time in med-

itation and reflection as you consider how to respond.

6. Write your thoughts and responses in the space provided in the study guide. This will help you to express your understanding of the passage clearly.

7. It might help to have a Bible dictionary handy. Use it to look up any unfamiliar words, names or places. (For additional help on how to study a passage, see chapter five of *Leading Bible Discussions,* InterVarsity Press.)

8. Consider how you can apply the Scripture to your life. Remember that the group will follow your lead in responding to the studies. They will not go any deeper than you do.

9. Once you have finished your own study of the passage, familiarize yourself with the leader's notes for the study you are leading. These are designed to help you in several ways. First, they tell you the purpose the study guide author had in mind when writing the study. Take time to think through how the study questions work together to accomplish that purpose. Second, the notes provide you with additional background information or suggestions on group dynamics for various questions. This information can be useful when people have difficulty understanding or answering a question. Third, the leader's notes can alert you to potential problems you may encounter during the study.

10. If you wish to remind yourself of anything mentioned in the leader's notes, make a note to yourself below that question in the study.

Leading the Study

1. Begin the study on time. Open with prayer, asking God to help the group to understand and apply the passage.

2. Be sure that everyone in your group has a study guide. Encourage the group to prepare beforehand for each discussion by reading the introduction to the guide and by working through the questions in the study.

3. At the beginning of your first time together, explain that these studies are meant to be discussions, not lectures. Encourage the members of the group to participate. However, do not put pressure on those who may be hesitant to speak during the first few sessions. You may want to suggest the following guidelines to your group.

■ Stick to the topic being discussed.

■ Your responses should be based on the verses which are the focus of the discussion and not on outside authorities such as commentaries or speakers.

■ These studies focus on a particular passage of Scripture. Only rarely should you refer to other portions of the Bible. This allows for everyone to participate in in-depth study on equal ground.

■ Anything said in the group is considered confidential and will not be discussed outside the group unless specific permission is given to do so.

■ We will listen attentively to each other and provide time for each person present to talk.

■ We will pray for each other.

4. Have a group member read the introduction at the beginning of the discussion.

5. Every session begins with a group discussion question. The question or activity is meant to be used before the passage is read. The question introduces the theme of the study and encourages group members to begin to open up. Encourage as many members as possible to participate, and be ready to get the discussion going with your own response.

This section is designed to reveal where our thoughts or feelings need to be transformed by Scripture. That is why it is especially important not to read the passage before the discussion question is asked. The passage will tend to color the honest reactions people would otherwise give because they are, of course, supposed to think the way the Bible does.

You may want to supplement the group discussion question with an icebreaker to help people to get comfortable. For more ideas, see Appendix A of *The Small-Group Leader* by John Mallison (Scripture Union).

You also might want to use the personal reflection question with your group. Either allow a time of silence for people to respond individually or discuss it together.

6. Have a group member (or members if the passage is long) read aloud the passage to be studied. Then give people several minutes to read the passage again silently so that they can take it all in.

7. Question 1 will generally be an overview question designed to briefly survey the passage. Encourage the group to look at the whole passage, but try to avoid getting sidetracked by questions or issues that will be addressed later in the study.

8. As you ask the questions, keep in mind that they are designed to be used just as they are written. You may simply read them aloud. Or you may prefer to express them in your own words.

There may be times when it is appropriate to deviate from the study guide. For example, a question may have already been answered. If so, move on to the next question. Or someone may raise an important question not covered in the guide. Take time to discuss it, but try to keep the group from going off on tangents.

9. Avoid answering your own questions. If necessary, repeat or rephrase them until they are clearly understood. Or point out something you read in the leader's notes to clarify the context or meaning. An eager group quickly becomes passive and silent if they think the leader will do most of the talking.

10. Don't be afraid of silence. People may need time to think about the question before formulating their answers.

11. Don't be content with just one answer. Ask, "What do the rest of you think?" or "Anything else?" until several people have given answers to the question.

12. Acknowledge all contributions. Try to be affirming whenever possible.

Never reject an answer. If it is clearly off-base, ask, "Which verse led you to that conclusion?" or again, "What do the rest of you think?"

13. Don't expect every answer to be addressed to you, even though this will probably happen at first. As group members become more at ease, they will begin to truly interact with each other. This is one sign of healthy discussion.

14. Don't be afraid of controversy. It can be very stimulating. If you don't resolve an issue completely, don't be frustrated. Move on and keep it in mind for later. A subsequent study may solve the problem.

15. Periodically summarize what the group has said about the passage. This helps to draw together the various ideas mentioned and gives continuity to the study. But don't preach.

16. At the end of the Bible discussion you may want to allow group members a time of quiet to work on an idea under "Now or Later." Then discuss what you experienced. Or you may want to encourage group members to work on these ideas between meetings. Give an opportunity during the session for people to talk about what they are learning.

17. Conclude your time together with conversational prayer, adapting the prayer suggestion at the end of the study to your group. Ask for God's help in following through on the commitments you've made.

18. End on time.

Many more suggestions and helps are found in *Leading Bible Discussions,* (InterVarsity Press, USA).

Components of Small Groups

A healthy small group should do more than study the Bible. There are four components to consider as you structure your time together.

Nurture. Small groups help us to grow in our knowledge and love of God. Bible study is the key to making this happen and is the foundation of your small group.

Community. Small groups are a great place to develop deep friendships with other Christians. Allow time for informal interaction before and after each study. Plan activities and games that will help you get to know each other. Spend time having fun together—going on a picnic or cooking dinner together.

Worship and prayer. Your study will be enhanced by spending time praising God together in prayer or song. Pray for each other's needs—and keep track of how God is answering prayer in your group. Ask God to help you to apply what you are learning in your study.

Outreach. Reaching out to others can be a practical way of applying what you are learning, and it will keep your group from becoming self-focused. Host a series of evangelistic discussions for your friends or neighbors. Clean up the yard of an elderly friend. Serve at a soup kitchen together, or spend a day working on a Habitat house.

Many more suggestions and helps in each of these areas are found in *Small Group Idea Book*. Information on building a small group can be found in *Small Group Leaders' Handbook* and *The Big Book on Small Groups* (both from Inter-Varsity Press) and *The Small-Group Leader* and *Small Group Starter Kit* (both from Scripture Union). Reading through one of these books would be worth your time.

Part 1: Serving in Home Territory. Luke 1:1—9:50.
General note. The first four studies could be grouped under the heading "God Breaks His Silence."

Study 1. Luke 1. People of Hope.
Purpose: To deepen our faith that God always fulfills his purposes and promises, and that he uses people of hope and obedience to do this.
General note. Extrabiblical studies keep confirming the historical accuracy of the third Gospel. Luke's own introduction is in classic Greek literary style (1:1-4). He claims to follow the principles of good history: acquaintance with similar accounts, interviews with primary sources—eyewitnesses and leading characters—investigation of reported events, orderliness in arranging materials and a clear aim.
Question 1. Do not linger on this question; it is intended mainly to get people to start looking at the text. Some possible reasons for God's choice: (1) Their priestly pedigree was not a decisive factor, but this detailed emphasis indicates they knew and appreciated their rich spiritual heritage (v. 5). (2) Being "righteous" does not mean they were morally perfect, but that their basic trust was in God's grace, not their own works. (3) They obeyed God's commands as best as they knew. (4) Zechariah had long been praying for the Messiah to come (v. 13).
Question 2. (1) He is identified as Gabriel, a prominent angel in the Bible. (2) He meets Zechariah in the house of God. (3) His message is specific and harmonizes with scriptural prophecy. (4) His message is for Israel and not a subjective situation. (5) His prophecy is objectively fulfilled.
Question 4. The birth of the Messiah's forerunner had to be unmistakably God's doing, not man's manipulation in any way. Consider their advanced age, Elizabeth's barrenness, the sign of Zechariah's muteness, the witness of many people to the effects of his vision in the temple, the nine-month pregnancy itself and the given name of John ("gift of God"). All pointed to the grace of God.
Question 5. Every devout girl of Judah's tribe dreamed of being the Messiah's mother. Mary would have been typical. But (1) she is a teenaged peasant girl, not a priest like Zechariah; (2) she is not yet "fully married"; (3) Gabriel twice pronounces her favored by God, not unbelieving like Zechariah; (4) the

Holy Spirit, not a man, is to bring that new life; (5) her son would be a divine king.

Question 6. Compare Zechariah's "how" (v. 18) with Mary's "how" (v. 34): Zechariah questioned the very possibility; Mary questioned the method.

Question 8. Mary's praise song reflects Hannah's when she also gave birth to a special leader-son in unique circumstances (1 Sam 2:1-10). Through the inspiration of the Holy Spirit, Mary modified it for her situation.

Question 9. Luke loves to describe happy family and community scenes. Here he starts this subtheme in his Gospel: people who witness or participate in God's wondrous works naturally tell others about it. (See note for question 5 above.) But at this point Luke seems especially eager to give objective witness to this supernatural event.

Study 2. Luke 2. Child of Hope.

Purpose: To experience afresh the wonder of the incarnation of God among us.

Question 1. Joseph had to take the weeklong trip to Bethlehem by foot with Mary about ready to give birth to a baby that was not his. Mary would be feeling physically uncomfortable, deeply concerned for her unusual child and tempted to worry about the future. In crowded Bethlehem there is no normal room in the inn, only space with the animals, possibly in the back of the inn.

Question 2. Luke has no need to embellish this awesome event. He lets the facts speak for themselves.

Question 3. Moving about the country as they did, shepherds were known for thievery and unreliability. Moreover, other Jews despised them because they were unable to keep the laws on ceremonial cleanness. These particular shepherds, however, indicate some kind of Old Testament faith about the coming of the Christ. They saw and heard not just one angel but a great company of angels. Luke's Gospel of grace shows us how social rejects were the first to hear of the birth of God's Son.

Question 4. They are trusting of God and one another. They are strong-willed, reflective and practical, realistic and hopeful. They are working together to fulfill God's will.

Question 5. Jesus means "he who saves." See Matthew 1:21.

Question 6. Jesus is about forty days old, judging by the time of Mary's purification. Simeon and Anna are, like Zechariah and Elizabeth, also aged, devout Old Testament believers who have waited a lifetime for the Messiah. They both immediately recognize the baby Jesus as that Messiah. Simeon's prophecy is to the parents. Anna's is to other faithful believers. Simeon's prophecy is long and detailed, including the remarkable prophecy about inclusion of the Gentiles. Specifically to Mary he prophesies that her son will be Israel's controversial Savior and that she must endure great pain.

Question 7. (1) He has a curious, probing mind—"sitting . . . listening . . .

asking them questions." Think of the implications as you picture Jesus at each activity! (2) He is respectful of his elders. (3) He is not being snippy in his response to Mary. Rather, his reference to "my Father" shows his awareness of a special relationship and loyalty to God that they do not yet fully understand. He is nevertheless obedient to them.

Study 3. Luke 3:1-20. Preacher of Hope.

Purpose: To seriously consider John's ministry of repentance as one that we much need today

Question 1. Luke likes to contrast earthly and heavenly authorities in introducing historic events (1:5; 2:1-3). Here again he helps us see that worldly governments often seem all-powerful to us, but that God is sovereign over them and over how history works out. Luke has introduced Jesus' eternal kingdom in 1:33, and he will progressively report Jesus' claims of this divine kingdom.

Question 2. When we repent, we accept the reality that we are sinful rebels against God, and we show hope that God wants to help us start all over again to find a truly fulfilled life.

Question 4. John is attacking the sin of materialism, which shows up when we trust in possessions for fulfillment and when we become greedy in acquiring them. Opposite to running after earthly goods is trusting God for fulfillment and true security. This basic sin of materialism does not only hurt others, it twists our lives. Jesus' teachings expand this subject (Lk 6:20-26; 12:13-34; 16:1-31).

Question 5. John presents a Christ far more powerful than himself, because the Christ will come as eternal judge, going beyond the baptizing of repentance to baptizing with the Holy Spirit and the fire of judgment. One needs to visualize John's metaphors to realize how fearful this Christ is!

Question 6. Like repentance, the warnings of God's coming judgment of sin are full of hope. It means that God is greater than the evil around us. The ministries of John and Jesus stress that there is an escape from this inevitable crisis. Do something about it now, before it is indeed too late. That's hope! That's good news!

Question 8. John had godly parents who obeyed the Scriptures. But he himself had to be steeped in the Law and the Prophets by the disciplines of study and long reflection (1:80). He was totally dedicated to God's service (1:15). He accepted his role as the Messiah's herald, no more, no less (3:15-17). He was a prophet of vision, discipline and passion.

Study 4. Luke 3:21—4:13. Hope for All People.

Purpose: To understand the authenticity of Jesus' humanity as our model in facing temptation.

General note. Don't read the genealogy aloud. Question 4 deals with it.

Question 1. Jesus was not baptized because he needed forgiveness of sin (compare v. 3). Rather, by this public act he identified with us in our need of repentance and forgiveness. Luke's focus is the Father's public approval of his Son as he begins his work. This was important both to Jesus and to the crowd (whether or not they understood the phenomena).

Question 3. By sandwiching this genealogy between his baptism and his temptation, Luke again stresses Jesus' universal humanity (see Heb 2:14-18; 5:7-9). In contrast, Matthew's genealogy of Jesus (1:1-16) begins with Abraham, father of the Jews, stresses his royal lineage from King David and ends with Joseph, "the husband of Mary." Luke's genealogy begins with Joseph and moves backward to Adam, paving the way for his dominant theme that Jesus' salvation is for the whole world, not only the Jews.

Question 4. The three natural and basic desires the devil appealed to were (1) to be physically comfortable, (2) to have and control things, and (3) to be accepted by and influence others. In verses 3 and 9 *if* (in Greek) equals "since," for the devil knew Jesus was God's Son. He also knew the basics of Jesus' mission: (1) God had given him power to help people; (2) God's aim was to regain his lost world by Jesus' death; (3) God's will is for people to follow him because they have changed from the inside out. Satan tried to make him compromise God's plans for him.

Question 5. The devil's appeals to Jesus were as follows: (1) "Use your powers to satisfy yourself as well as to help people." (2) "You don't have to gain the world by dying on the cross. Do it my way; it's easier. Just give me your loyalty." (3) "Getting people to change morally is the slow way. Do something sensational and people will follow you."

Question 6. It's clear to see how Jesus met each temptation: with appropriate Scripture. But he didn't come by this overnight.

Study 5. Luke 4:14—5:16. Outrageous Claims.

Purpose: To value Jesus' claims to be God's Messiah and to see their direct relevance to us as his subjects

General note. We can see a link to the previous section in several ways: (1) Jesus' victory over Satan's temptations makes him determined to serve God well as he begins his mission. (2) He is filled with the power of the Spirit to do that work (see also 3:21; 4:1). (3) The testings prepare him better for both the popularity and the hostility that are coming.

Studies five through seven could be grouped under the heading "The King Has Arrived!"

Question 4. They are initially impressed with Jesus' eloquence and authority. But their prejudices flare up when he talks about God blessing Gentiles, not Israel, in Old Testament events they know well. He doesn't fit their idea of God's Messiah. He's just the town carpenter. They know his family background—and something about his birth which most of them probably interpreted as illegitimate. How dare he make such a great claim to be the Messiah!

Question 6. He controls the activities, not the other way around. Each activity is inspired by high motivation to help people, not to promote self. He knows when to stop and be recharged by God. (The parallel text of Mark 1:35 says he went to the solitary place to pray.) He is clear why he is working that way and knows when to move on.

Question 8. Be sure these progressive steps are clear so the group can answer the question: (1) Jesus goes to Simon's workplace. (2) He uses Simon's boat as part of his teaching ministry. (3) Right afterward he gives Simon a hard command. (4) He listens to but doesn't argue with Simon's objection. (5) Jesus lets Simon and his partners work out the miraculous catch of fish. (6) Simon, the big fisherman, is caught!

Question 9. (1) He is known for helping outcasts. (2) He has compassion for people and relates to them as individuals. (3) He does not fear contamination but risks becoming unclean himself. (4) He is decisive. (5) He keeps the sensible community laws. (6) He habitually prays.

Study 6. Luke 5:17—6:11. Opposition to Authority.

Purpose: To see how religious leaders oppose Jesus' messianic claim and to learn from him how to meet criticisms.

Question 1. From verses 15-17 it is clear that Jesus' reputation has become so widespread that representative authorities from every corner of the nation come to Galilee to check him out. (Again, note Luke's love for contrasting these earthly powers with the power of the Lord.) The group should begin to anticipate knockdown, dragged-out controversies.

Question 2. (1) People everywhere are "amazed at his teaching because his message had authority" (4:31). Both Mark (1:22) and Matthew (7:29) add "not like their teachers of the law." So their positions as revered biblical scholars are at stake. (2) He is challenging their traditional interpretations of the law. (3) He is gaining more disciples.

Question 3. Assign one episode each to individuals or partners to think through.

Verses	Jesus' Radical Activities	Assumptions Jesus Challenges
5:17-26	He claimed authority to forgive sin.	Jesus is not God. It is not possible for God to become man.
5:27-28	He called an outcast to be his disciple.	Only pious people join a good religious leader. Jesus cannot possibly be such a leader.
5:29-32	He socialized with crooks and immoral community rejects.	These people are beyond redemption. Jesus must be like them, since birds of a feather flock together.

| 5:33-39 | He led a positive, joyful lifestyle with his disciples. | Religion, like God, is joyless, a matter of somber ritual and pious behavior. |
| 6:1-11 | He worked on the sabbath to help heal people. | Sabbath rest means minimal work, not even helping needy people when you can. |

Question 4. They alternately criticize Jesus and his disciples, but their target is always Jesus. They begin with internal questions, then raise direct questions, make specific charges and end with deliberately waiting to make official charges and determination to destroy him.

Study 7. Luke 6:12-49. Character of Kingdom Citizens.

Purpose: To examine the character and lifestyle Jesus requires of his people and to measure ourselves against his standard and example.

General note. Jesus' "Sermon on the Plain" in Luke is a condensed version of Matthew's Sermon on the Mount (chaps. 5-7). But Luke means his Beatitudes to be a more literal, physical way than Matthew's spiritual Beatitudes. So both are complementary.

The materials in this section lend themselves to several studies because the group may find more to discuss on these practical topics. But sticking to the major questions here will help them see the bigger picture of Jesus' intentions, not just isolated moral principles.

Question 1. (1) Jesus' immense popularity meant he needed close partners for the work. (2) The intensifying hostility also meant Jesus needed to train associates to take over his work. (3) By this time (the beginning of the second year) both Jesus and the disciples had had enough opportunity for mutual observation. (4) There were evidently hundreds of them to choose from. So he had to weigh all choices carefully. (5) Jesus was ready to present in a more formal way the high standards of his kingdom and would need deeply committed coworkers.

Other considerations not from the immediate context: (1) His team would need a mixture of temperaments and characters. (2) Knowing Scripture predictions of a traitor, he may well have had struggles. (3) He wanted to be clear about his Father's guidance in these strategic choices.

Question 2. Luke makes it clear that Jesus is addressing his startling discourse to his disciples (vv. 20-22). The others are eavesdropping on what he says must characterize citizens of his kingdom.

Question 3. Everyone is driven by need for security. The average worldly person is not spiritual-minded. His or her security is in the visible material goods that bring position, power, prestige. Jesus' standards are upside-down values to the typical worldling.

Question 4. Jesus draws a sharp contrast between the two lifestyles and their destiny. He appeals to his disciples to take the long-range perspective. The materialistic, hedonistic lifestyle may be attractive but is shortsighted, for at the end of the day it has self-destructed (cf. his parable in Lk 12:13-21).

The Disciples' Lifestyle	The Worldling's Lifestyle
Now poor in material goods but possessing God's kingdom	Now rich in material goods but no comfort (security) later
Now hungry but satisfied later	Now well-fed but hungry later
Now weeping but laughing later	Now laughing but mourning and weeping later
Now persecuted but rewarded in heaven	Now praised by men but rejected by God

Question 6. (1) It stops the vicious cycle of hate (vv. 27-29). (2) It develops a generous character (v. 30). (3) It promotes mutual care (v. 31). (4) Disciples must live by a higher standard than sinners (vv. 32-34). (5) Disciples will be greatly rewarded by developing a character like God's—generous, gracious, kind, merciful (vv. 35-36).

Question 7. When you judge others (1) be forgiving; (2) be generous; (3) keep in mind you will be judged by the same way you judge others; (4) check your own faults.

Question 10. Be prepared to deal personally with anyone who needs individual help on this last question.

Study 8. Luke 7. Five Kinds of Faith.

Purpose: To discern how differently people express faith, and to learn from Jesus how to interact sensitively with different people.

General note. Studies eight through eleven could be grouped under the heading "Jesus Draws Out Faith."

Question 1. The centurion is a Roman military officer, so to the Jews he's a despised Gentile. Widows in those days had a very rough time if they had no male relative to defend them. They were generally considered second-class citizens. This widow, however, is accompanied by a "large crowd from the town" (v. 12). John the Baptist's background is religiously impeccable, but he is now a political prisoner. Simon belonged to the most influential religious party in Israel then. The woman was a prostitute, possibly a well-paid one.

Question 2. This question has clear textual answers, so don't let it be mechanically answered. It's a way of getting the group to observe the text.

Question 3. In Jesus' miraculous works someone always had faith—the person asking for help, friends or family bringing a loved one to Jesus, or Jesus himself. The widow is too immersed in her sorrow to even think that there could be a change. Here Jesus expresses his faith in practical compassion. He doesn't wait to be asked, and this is how he continues to work today if we have even the minimum of passive faith, as the woman may have had.

Question 5. What a contrast between John in prison and John at the River

Jordan! The longer he languishes in Herod's dungeon, the greater his doubts grow that Jesus is the Messiah. Jesus' message to John was not just some Bible verses or a lecture on how to have faith behind bars. He sends John's disciples back with hard evidence that he was doing exactly what the Messiah was supposed to be doing. Compare the list in Isaiah 61:1-2, which he had claimed earlier in Luke 4:18-19.

Question 6. Education may stuff people with knowledge but doesn't necessarily make them wise. It's making the best use of knowledge learned that makes one truly educated. As we saw in study six, the men were frozen in their prejudices and traditional beliefs. To give these up would threaten their religious security and leadership status with its prestige and privileges. "My mind is made up. Don't confuse me with facts." That's how Jesus seems to be describing their mentality.

Question 8. The woman's faith in Jesus is obvious. But Simon also shows signs of some faith in Jesus (vv. 36, 39-40, 43). (1) He addresses Simon by name (not Jesus' usual practice). (2) He dialogues with him. (3) He arouses his curiosity. (4) He appeals to him as a Pharisee on an intellectual level. (5) He involves him in the lesson with a question. (6) He uses the immediate situation as a living parable.

Question 9. Jesus knows that the woman has a strong intuitive nature, not an intellectual approach to life. She understands actions and can sense rather than rationally evaluate people's thoughts and feelings. On the other hand, Jesus appeals to Simon as the educated intellectual that Pharisees were. He uses reasoning, questions, debating points, parabolic language, immediate illustrations, comparisons, contrasts and finally, hard application.

Question 10. Some possible answers are that John had doubting, shaking, disappointed faith. The woman had extravagant, lavish, grateful faith, while Simon had cautious, mustard-seed faith.

Study 9. Luke 8:1-21. Hearing God: First Step of Faith.

Purpose: To be convinced of the importance of hearing God's Word well and practicing it seriously.

Question 1. These women have interesting and varied backgrounds. They are evidently wealthy enough to support Jesus and the disciples.

Question 2. To be Jesus' disciple one must take time to hear what God is really saying through his Word (not just what one remembers from years past) and to put it into practice.

Question 3. The soils vary in viability: hardened soil, which the seeds cannot even penetrate; rocky soil, which accepts the seeds but cannot nourish them for long; thorny soil, which has more soil than the second so that the seeds grow into plants but do not mature into fruitfulness because the competing roots of the thorn suck up the soil's nutrients; good soil.

Question 4. Good location, proper amount of sun and water, fertilizers, constant weeding, TLC.

Questions 5-6. These questions, like others throughout this guide, are quite personal. They're intended to draw out people's problems and encourage honesty about their lives. Bible study must be personal and practical. People who join a Bible study want to share and get practical help and prayer. But, of course, the leader must watch that no one dominates.

Question 7. If Mary and her other sons heard what Jesus said in verse 21, they could have felt put down. But that's the hard point that Jesus is making: family connections do not assure one's entry into the kingdom of God. Again, what God looks for are faithful hearers and doers.

Question 8. See also Luke 12:51-53 and John 7:2-5.

Study 10. Luke 8:22-56. Jesus' Identity: Bedrock of Faith.

Purpose: To reconsider how well we know Jesus and his active power in our world.

General note. For about a year the disciples have watched and heard an extraordinary man saying and doing extraordinary things. But they don't yet know his full identity as God. These four power events are linked topically, chronologically and geographically. Only the disciples witness all four, and it only gradually dawns on them who Jesus really is. The power encounters move progressively to the climax, pointing to the fact he is Lord of life and death. About a year later they confess he is God's Messiah (Mt 16:16; Lk 9:18-20).

Question 1. All are tired after listening to Jesus teach publicly all day and then explain his teachings to them in private (Mark 4:1-35). So they must be feeling relieved and glad to get away for rest. The sudden storm brings fear and panic, perhaps anger at Jesus. The event concludes with a different kind of fear.

Question 2. Make full use of this personal question. It can help not only seekers but also Christians who are vague in their understanding of Jesus Christ the Lord.

Question 3. (1) The account is very detailed. (2) They are in foreign territory. (3) The man (or more likely the demon) immediately recognizes Jesus' true identity. (4) The man does not ask to be delivered but to not be tortured. (5) There are references to one evil spirit and then to many evil spirits controlling the man. (6) Jesus deals successively with the man and then with all the demons. (7) The demons beg repeatedly that Jesus not send them into the Abyss (Rev. 9:1-3).

Question 4. Some suggestions include: they don't want anyone upsetting their lucrative pork and leather business; the normalization of the crazed man upsets their stability (like the police not wanting to clean up a red light district); they sense that Jesus wants to change their lives, and they don't want that to happen.

Question 5. (1) Her condition is described in unusual detail. (2) She approaches Jesus surreptitiously, for she is a ritually unclean person (Lev 15:25-31). (3) She is healed without a face-to-face encounter with him. (4) Her faith seems to be in touching Jesus' cloak. (5) Jesus stubbornly insists on knowing who touched him.

Question 6. One possible suggestion is that he wants to clarify her faith—not in his cloak but in himself. Another suggestion is that he wants the people to accept her as a healed "daughter," no longer a religious outcast. Another reason may be that Jesus wants his disciples to learn more about helping people.

Question 8. He can control the violence of nature. He can control the violence of evil. He can heal an incurable physical affliction. He can raise up dead people. It's beginning to sink into their consciousness that Jesus is Lord over all of life and death!

Question 9. For instance, (1) people are in deep trouble. (2) They make every human effort to solve their problem. (3) Death is the next stage. (4) The people desperately appeal to Jesus. (5) Jesus takes time to converse with them. (6) His power alone takes them out of the crisis. (7) Jesus always encourages their faith. (8) Things get back to normal.

Study 11. Luke 9:1-50. Disciple Training: Stretched in Faith.

Purpose: To take a closer look at how Jesus trained his disciples and follow his example for training the next generation of leaders for our churches.

General note. In their first year the disciples mainly watch Jesus as he ministers to people all over Galilee. In the second year Jesus chooses twelve from among the many disciples and exposes them to special revelatory events. They begin to ask questions. Now at the start of the third year he sends them out on their first evangelistic mission. Their training will grow harder. The group questions aim to help people probe the example of Jesus as a leader of leaders, a trainer of trainers to carry on his world mission.

Question 1. Jesus set the example by (1) being open to help anyone and everyone; (2) relating to people as valuable individuals; (3) taking risks in ministry and letting go of useless traditions; (4) depending on God for everything; (5) not letting official opposition stop their work; (6) focusing on God's kingdom and not material security; (7) being in constant touch with the Father.

Question 3. Jesus (1) counters their negative reaction with positive action (v. 13); (2) engages them in discussion about solving the problem (v. 13); (3) involves them in working with him, beginning with a simple task (vv. 14-15); (4) multiplies the resources himself but makes them distribute the food (v. 16); (5) concludes the training in a practical way (v. 17).

Question 4. Jesus promises his followers they will save their true life, share his glory when he returns and see the kingdom of God. We can see this cost-benefit principle when people succeed in worthwhile goals after sacrificing an easy lifestyle and enduring hard disciplines—a sports champion, a scholarship winner, a concert pianist, a doctor and so on.

Question 6. Luke links Jesus' transfiguration to his death mission in Jerusalem (9:30-32, 51). The disciples still do not grasp this death mission (vv. 22, 31), but a few months later they will be able to recall this visual, audible experience and take hope again.

Jesus' transfiguration stressed his mission with God's purposes in the Old Testament, previewed his ultimate glory, which would be achieved only after his death, and reinforced his resolve to go to Jerusalem to accomplish his death mission for humanity's salvation.

Question 7. The first is selective hearing that screens out what they don't want to hear (vv. 44-45). The second is rivalry among themselves (vv. 46-48). The third is exclusivism (vv. 49-50).

Question 8. Their strong self-orientation and big egos were expressed in (1) growing rivalry among the themselves, (2) mistrust of each other's motives the closer they get to Jerusalem and anticipated glory (who would get the highest cabinet posts in Jesus' national government?), and (3) a growing sense of superiority to people not as close to Jesus as them.

Part 2: The Way to Jerusalem

General note. During this final third year Jesus spends more and more time in training the Twelve, both in teaching and practical assignments. As they move up to Jerusalem more people want to be his disciples. He clarifies what it means to follow him. The title of each lesson on this topic reflects the response of superficial would-be followers.

The first five studies in this section could be grouped under the heading "Jesus Sets the Price for Discipleship."

Study 12. Luke 9:51—10:24. God Asks Too Much.

Purpose: To be able to recognize and do something about cheap discipleship in our churches and in ourselves.

Group discussion. As with other opening questions to bridge the text to relevance, this one is quite personal. Sometimes it primes the pump if the leader shares his or her own experience—as long as it does not overwhelm by length or drama.

Question 2. (1) God loves Samaritans as much as he loves Jews. (2) Evangelize those outside your own ethnic group. (3) Don't get discouraged by racial hostility. (4) Don't stay where you're not wanted. (5) Jesus is the Lord of the harvest, not us.

Question 3. *Earthly values*: The first candidate thinks that following Jesus is going to be a ball. He is Mr. Too Quick. Jesus' response is to divest him of physical/material expectations. *Cultural values*: To a second candidate Jesus initiates the call to follow him, indicating he perceived the man's potential. But he is Mr. Too Slow, one who agrees following Jesus is a good idea—but only after he has fulfilled his culture's norm of an oldest son's obligations. *Social values (peer pressure)*: Mr. Two Hearts has the enthusiasm of Mr. Too Quick. But like Mr. Too Slow he also has his precondition: he will follow Jesus after his social obligations to his extended family back home. *Jesus calls for total commitment.* None of the three grasp the self-sacrifice that Jesus asks of his disciples.

Question 4. (1) Here Jesus sends out seventy-two disciples, probably including the Twelve. (2) His first instruction is to pray for more workers because of the plentiful harvest (among the Gentiles). (3) He sends them out two by two. (4) His instructions are more extensive. (5) They are not to greet anyone on the road (no time for the long Middle Eastern greetings). (6) They are not to be fussy about room and board. (7) Warnings about rejection by towns are more detailed. (8) Jesus' last word: You represent me.

Question 6. We also need Jesus' caution when, like the seventy-two, we are successful in our ministries. We can get puffed up with self-importance and triumphalism. We may begin to think we did it by our own power. We can lose sight of God's grace in salvation, and we can become activistic in short-term projects and forget to be reflective at Jesus' feet.

Question 7. Jesus further rejoices because God's wisdom has been shown to simple believers as his evangelists, and not necessarily to sophisticated scholars, and the success of the seventy-two disciples is evidence that they can eventually carry on his mission without his physical presence.

Study 13. Luke 10:25—11:13. Rituals or Relationships?

Purpose: To develop habits and activities that strengthen our personal relationship with God and to reexamine the place of rituals in our religion.

Question 1. The "expert of the law" (NIV) or "lawyer" (NRSV) represented Israel's top biblical scholars. They were often associated with the Pharisees, who were self-appointed watchdogs to preserve the Old Testament laws. This one has a courteous manner, addressing Jesus as "Teacher." He asks a good question. He has good answers, for which Jesus commends him. Though he is defensive and self-justifying, he is willing to listen further to Jesus.

Question 2. This expert was typical of his class in knowing well the letter of the law but not its living experience. Jesus challenges him to personal application twice—directly (vv. 28, 37) and indirectly but powerfully through the parable.

Question 3. Don't spiritualize the physical details as some have done. For instance, allegorists have interpreted the oil as the Holy Spirit and the wine as the blood of Jesus. These were a traveler's first-aid kit. Two silver coins (two days wages) paid for a week at the inn. Jesus' detailed description shows how methodical, personal and thorough was the Samaritan's practical care for the dying man, down to "I'll return to check up on his progress and take care of additional expenses."

Jesus challenges the expert's religion through a parable. He unexpectedly portrays the hero as a despised Samaritan. He is a sharp contrast to the priest and Levite, who are professionals in the institutional religion that the expert represents.

Question 4. Jesus' aim is to teach the expert how to put the law into action. He challenges him not to debate who his neighbor is, but *to be a neighbor* to needy people around him. He is (we are) to demonstrate the right relationship with God by having a right relationship with people. We are to love and help people in practical ways, just as Jesus did.

Question 8. Matthew 6:9-13 has the longer and more commonly used version, which we use here. The "prayer headings" are the person and nature of God (v. 9), the purposes of God (v. 10), the provisions of God (vv. 11-13) and the power of God.

Question 9. The first picture portrays God as a friend who delights in giving, not a reluctant friend who finally gives only so he can go back to sleep. The second portrays God as a father who delights in giving the best to his children.

Study 14. Luke 11:14—12:12. No, Not That Jesus.
Purpose: To learn from Jesus to hate falsehood and stand for truth with passion.

Question 1. Jesus' driving out a mute demon is a spectacular miracle. The crowd is impressed. Jesus' critics cannot deny the reality of Jesus' power. But two groups of critics use diversionary tactics to undermine his authority. Neither group accepts Jesus' exorcism as a sign of divine authority, even though people generally did. The first attacking group tries to minimize the effect of the miracle by explaining that Jesus' power came from Satan. The second group also wants to divert attention by asking for a further show of signs, as though the miracle was not at all impressive.

Question 2. That he is Satan's ally doesn't make sense, because delivering people from demons is destroying Satan's work! Satan would be working against his kingdom/house to give Jesus power to drive out demons.

Question 3. This controversy gives Jesus opportunity to make clear that he has come to defeat evil, Satan's kingdom of darkness. His claims: He is the stronger man who defeats the strong man (Satan) guarding his possessions (people under his control; 11:21-22). Jesus' presence calls for a decisive choice: One must be for or against the kingdom of God (personal kingship of Jesus). There can be no neutrality in the battle against evil (11:23). When Jesus, the victorious King, overpowers Satan, he thoroughly defeats evil. His is not a temporary moral reformation (11:24-26). In his kingdom what matters is not physical relationships but obedience to the word of God (11:27-38).

Question 4. Jesus is saying he is greater than the prophet Jonah and King Solomon, both of whom his listeners were proud of. They both had Gentile audiences who responded to their message positively. (Compare Luke 4:24-27, where Jesus also deliberately used similar illustrations about Gentile responsiveness to God's message.) He calls his critics a wicked generation. He compares them unfavorably with the Gentile queen of the south (1 Kings 10:1-10) and the thoroughly pagan Ninevites (Jon 3), both of whom acknowledged the truth upon hearing it.

Question 6. Jesus' six woes, part of his controversy here (11:42-53), are taken up in "Now or Later."

Question 7. Jesus' disciples need never fear persecution from other human beings, no matter how powerful they may be in the world. That is cowardly fear, for God is far greater than them and controls them. The proper kind of fear is the awesome respect for the sovereign God. Fear God, and you need fear nothing else.

Study 15. Luke 12:13—13:21. Hey, I Want to Enjoy Life Now.

Purpose: To check whether our lifestyle and priorities are earthbound or eternal, and to see if our ideas of enjoying life are short-sighted or far-sighted.

General note. This study is long. You may want to encourage people to study the "Now or Later" material on their own.

Question 1. Jesus addresses the crowd because he knows that the average person is like the man, bent on amassing possessions rather than finding real life. So he is referring to all kinds of greed—scams, competitors secretly agreeing to keep prices high, embezzling, tax evasions, going to sales not because of need but to find bargains, keeping things you haven't used for years and so on.

Question 2. Twenty-four hours a day, year in and year out he sees only his possessions. All his time and energies are spent on acquiring more and more. The repetitious use of *I, my* and *myself* stresses his total self-absorption. The absence of any other human being in the story is spooky. He talks only to himself! He relates to things, not people. His materialism has made him a subhuman being—alone and with nothing at the end.

Question 3. People are fools when they focus only on this temporal, material life and make no plan for eternal life. People are fools when they love things and use people to get more things. People are fools when they play God.

Question 4. Their God is evidently uncaring, remote, indifferent to his creatures. Jesus' Father is exactly the opposite!

Question 6. Jesus is using the then-familiar household responsibility of the manager to look after the welfare of other servants. He represents church leaders today. He is to treat them as though the master were physically present. The scene in verse 45 was not uncommon! Negligence of greater responsibility brings greater punishment (v. 46).

Question 8. The three changing scenes that are signs of coming judgment are dysfunctional/divided homes, a weather station and a courtroom. The courtroom of judgment is the climax. Jesus is appealing to those in the crowd, interested but still unrepentant: The end is near! Repent before it's too late.

Question 12. The ruler's concern is following the traditional legalistic rules of sabbath observance. Jesus is concerned with helping people to be whole, not maintaining meaningless and even cruel observances. By touching the crippled woman (possibly with a spinal bone fusion or muscular paralysis), he rendered himself ritually unclean. When he berates the ruler he is challenging officialdom. He gives dignity to the woman, calling her a daughter of Abraham, thus appealing to others to accept her as one of them.

Question 13. The mustard seed in Palestine is almost invisible to the casual eye but can grow into a mini-tree eight to ten feet high with strong branches. Likewise, the yeast is invisible compared to the amount of flour it affects. This is the nature of God's kingdom. The beginning is slow and unseen but sure and pervasive. Jesus is saying that his kingdom has been facing opposition—its values clash with earthly values—but in the end its triumph will be visible.

Study 16. Luke 13:22—14:35. Three Surprises in Heaven.

Purpose: To sharpen our understanding of who qualifies for eternal life with God, and to be more effective in our witness to others about God's salvation.

Question 1. Jesus' listeners would have been shocked that the owner of the house (God) seems so inhospitable, harsh and unfair, not acknowledging people who claim to be his associates (Israel) (13:24-27), and that not only the VIPs of Israel but also Gentiles will feast in the kingdom of God, while self-designated guests are thrown out (13:28-30).

Question 2. Suggestions: (1) For good reasons a pilot has only a narrow strip on which to land his plane safely, not just any field. (2) For the survival of their patients, expert doctors have a carefully considered method of saving them, not just any kind of therapy. (3) God's kingdom is a monarchy, not a democracy. (4) Christians did not think up these conditions; the omniscient God did.

Question 3. The Pharisees' motive for warning Jesus is not clear (13:31). But it's interesting that they are now allied with the Herodians, their political enemies, against Jesus. He is totally fearless (13:31-33).

Like all faithful Jews, Jesus loved Jerusalem, but not for nationalistic reasons. For him it was the historic, spiritual city of God. From Jerusalem should have flowed God's salvation for the whole world. Instead, he predicts, it will be destroyed because it has been ingrown and disobedient (21:20-24). Politically, the anti-Roman Pharisees hated the pro-Roman Herods, who were not pure Jews but Idumean, and in power only because of their subservience to Rome. See also Mark 3:6, an early indication of their deadly alliance against Jesus.

"Today . . . tomorrow and . . . the third day" was a Jewish figure of speech, meaning a given period of time.

Question 4. They were in a dilemma with Jesus' first question (14:3). They could not have defended either a yes or a no answer. Everyone knew that was exactly what they did on the sabbath day (14:5). Jesus' authority in logic and practical experience shut their mouths.

Question 5. Notice the drive for social status/recognition to the disregard of others (14:7-11) and the selfish use of hospitality for mutual benefit.

Question 6. Those who will be saved are not people who, like the once privileged associates of the wedding host (Israel), dishonor God by making light of his invitation to celebrate with him, but rather people who, like the final guests (Gentiles), know they are undeserving but are persuaded by the grace of the divine host.

Question 8. Jesus is using a violent analogy to illustrate his condition for discipleship.

Criminals shouldering wooden cross beams from the capital to a hill of execution right outside was not an unusual sight. Jeering mobs usually accompanied them. Crucifixion was the most agonizing form of execution, a slow death that could last up to four days. So the thinking listener that day would have understood the metaphor as "You have to put yourself to death."

Study 17. Luke 15. Parable of Two Lost Sons.

Purpose: To nurture a deeper appreciation of God's rejoicing nature and to improve our relationships to God and other members of his family.

General note. Studies seventeen through nineteen could be grouped under the heading "Jesus Tells the Greatest Stories Ever Heard."

Question 1. Jesus' association with tax collectors and immoral people deeply offended the religious leaders. Pharisees (nonprofessional religious leaders) and teachers of the law (professional) have been hounding Jesus since the beginning (5:17). He has made his judgment on them (7:30-35; 11:37-52). But they are relentless in their attacks, as we just saw in chapter 14.

Question 2. The unusual length and details of the third parable tell us that Jesus has been building up to this climax. While the first two deal with non-human values, this one deals with human values—family/community ties and personal relationships. The third goes beyond the lost-and-found motif to a second theme of broken relationships and the reasons for such.

Question 3. Let this well-known parable challenge the group to move beyond familiar sentiments to fresh insights. This question can help the group to go beyond the fact that the younger son simply has a drop-dead-Dad attitude in asking for his inheritance while the father is still alive. What could have led up to this shocking request? For example, he had had enough of his older brother's bossing him around. He had little to look forward to hanging around home. Don't speculate too much, just enough to understand the younger son's situation in a warm, human way.

Question 4. This further probes question 3. It gives opportunity for people to identify with the younger son in positive ways. For example, he was adventurous. He wanted to experience life with a capital L. He was willing to take risks. Some people can only learn from experience. But don't stay too long on this question (or question 3).

Question 5. "Coming to his senses" doesn't necessarily mean repentance, as some think. Consider how self-serving his plans are (vv. 17-18) and what condition he wants to propose (v. 19). But it is the start of his turnabout. Genuine repentance is never a sudden, spontaneous experience. The theme of repentance crops up here and throughout Luke: 3:3-8; 5:32; 10:13; 13:3-5 and thereafter. Be careful to treat this topic with respect, not superficiality. This is our Lord Jesus constantly holding out hope for people!

Question 6. The father has been waiting a long time for his son to return. (Peering down the road whenever he could?) For the father's (Jesus') compassionate attitude see Matthew 9:36; 14:14; 15:32; 18:27, 33; 20:34; Mark 1:41; Luke 7:13; 10:33. His actions at the end of verse 20 are most undignified and humiliating for a man of his status in the Middle East. He ignores the son's rehearsed speech and commands the greatest celebration possible (vv. 21–24).

Question 7. (1) He loves the elder son as much as his younger son. (2) He again acts in humiliation by going out and pleading with him. (3) He listens to the son's complaints and answers him positively. (4) He wants the elder son to be reconciled to his brother and to celebrate with the household. (5) He has hope for his elder son!

Study 18. Luke 16. Parables on Smart Money.

Purpose: To take on Jesus' perspective of managing our earthly resources of money, time and energies with eternity's values in view.

Question 2. This parable can be complicated because we must be clear that Jesus is not condoning greed and dishonesty. Here's one popular interpretation: Jesus is commending the shrewd manager for knowing how to use money to insure a secure future. He then applies that example to his disciples. As enlightened people they should be all the more wise in making the right investments to secure their eternal future. For instance, we are to use our earthly resources to help people enter heaven.

A cultural explanation is attractive to modern scholars like Leon Morris (*Luke,* IVP), K. E. Bailey (*Poet and Peasant Through Peasant Eyes,* Eerdmans) and I. Howard Marshall (*The Gospel of Luke,* Paternoster). It takes into account the commercial practices of that day. A manager could make personal profit on his master's debts by charging whatever interest he chose, as long as he returned the principal to his master. According to the Old Testament, this was legal, if not quite kosher, for a strict Jew. In our present manager's crisis he forfeited his personal profit while still collecting his manager's principal. He thus saved his master's reputation of being generous and insured himself a comfortable future by appreciative friends.

Question 3. Jesus does call the manager dishonest. But he broadens the idea of dishonesty far beyond stealing or embezzlement as it is usually understood. As he proceeds he shows that dishonesty with money is any misuse of money or possessions, for example, using them for personal benefit and not for people, or just keeping them to earn more money, or not using them at all.

Question 4. The manager has indeed been dishonest in squandering his master's possessions. Jesus' commentary is that we, as people of light who should know better, can also be dishonest when we use God-given resources wrongly. We are not smart in how we use our resources to guarantee our future with God. (1) We are only managers of God's money, not owners. (2) Wise investment of our resources is based on mutual trust between God, the owner, and us, the managers. (3) Good management leads to greater responsibility (v. 10). (Jesus expands this point in Luke 19:15-19.) (4) If we have mismanaged our material possessions, we can't be trusted with spiritual riches (vv. 10-12). (5) It is impossible to love both God and money at the same time.

Question 5. The Pharisees were supposed to be serving God, but they were known to love money. Jesus uses them as examples of the impossibility of serving both God and money (vv. 13-15). How bold to criticize them in public! But he knows how they twist the Scripture to justify their greed, as well as their rationalizations about Moses' law on divorce. Note how he upholds the sovereignty of God and his Word over them (vv. 15-18).

Question 7. He did not consider his riches as God's. They were his to spend as he pleased. And what pleased him was a lavish lifestyle. Purple and fine linen were equivalents of Armani suits and Versace underwear. "Living in luxury every day" meant having gourmet meals all the time. He was so self-absorbed that he never saw at his gate the filthy beggar Lazarus, who could have survived from just the crumbs dropped from his table.

Question 8. Abraham in this very Jewish parable represents God. To be at Abraham's side is symbolic of the best existence possible—with God. Lazarus did not deserve heaven because he was a beggar. The name Jesus gives him means "God is my helper"—his way of saying Lazarus's implicit faith was in God's grace. There is personal consciousness in life after death. Heaven and hell apparently are in view of one another but have no mutual access. Hell is torture and agony (because of regrets, lost opportunities, hopelessness, aloneness). Both are fixed conditions.

Question 9. In hell one has time to think of what, after all, was really most important on earth. The once-rich man never asks Abraham to deliver him from hell, for he knows he deserves hell. Hell is torment because one realizes the truth too late. Now in hell he learns too late that he did not obey the Scriptures (Moses and the Prophets) he had known, for Abraham (Jesus) makes clear that he could have had salvation from hell had he obeyed God's Word while on earth.

Study 19. Luke 17:1—18:14. Pictures of Hanging In There.

Purpose: To listen to Jesus' personal encouragement as we grow in faith, especially when we're in seemingly hopeless situations.

Question 1. Verse 5 may be a clue for tying together these seemingly unrelated teachings and events. The apostles seem to be telling Jesus, "What you're telling us to do takes faith we haven't got. Increase our faith!"

Question 2. In the first picture, the viability of a mustard seed to grow and mature to fruitfulness is not in its original size but in its nature to grow. So true faith by its nature grows. It is not measured by visible "size" (big words, emotional display) but by the quiet, invisible dependence on God who grows bigger and bigger in lives. The second picture demonstrates how our faith becomes weak or misplaced if we forget that ultimately we are servants to the King. When we think that God is there to serve our wishes, that's a pretty small god! (On the other hand, see what Jesus also says about this servant-master relation in Luke 12:37—an astonishing balance!)

Question 3. Thanklessness is a form of disregard for God, the Creator of our human nature and the source of all we have. Gratitude to him expresses healthy faith in a good, generous God. (Romans 1:21 shows the contrast, and 4:20 shows a remarkable example of how to grow faith.)

Question 4. Jesus had already talked about the coming of the kingdom of God (9:26; 10:9-11; 12:40). So naturally people were raising questions about the timing. He replies that the kingdom will not come with observable physical signs, but with spiritual discernment. "Within you [plural]" in verse 21 can also mean "among or in the midst of you, within your grasp." He obviously did not mean the kingdom was in the Pharisees to whom he was speaking. He is referring to his personal kingship (the kingdom of God) right in their midst and already in operation among his disciples.

Question 5. *Time* (January 18, 1999) reported that in the United States there are about two thousand to ten thousand cults, appealing to people with strange teachings and weird promises. Their followers are either very spiritually hungry or very naive. But think also of the authorities who have the last word in various fields, appealing to your health, your ambitions, your self-esteem (and think of the millions they're making). These messiahs can detract us from anticipating the King, the Son of Man (Dan 7:13-14).

Question 6. The metaphor of lightning stresses the sudden, unexpected, fear-inspiring but unmistakable coming of God's judgment, which here is equated with the return of the Son of Man (vv. 24, 30).

Question 7. When we get preoccupied with the powerful influences in our culture (mass media and its values, keeping up with the latest trends, celebrity worship, novel entertainment, Hollywood's standards, material satisfaction, professional competitiveness), they begin to suck up our time and energies. The people in the time of Noah and Lot knew of God's coming judgment way ahead of time, but it was sudden to them because they were preoccupied with earthly life. This is Jesus' warning to us today.

Question 8. Some possible reasons include: God doesn't answer quickly or in the way they would like. They may be asking for the wrong things or with the wrong motives. They didn't mean it. They have the wrong view of God and of prayer.

Question 9. (1) God is deeply interested in us, not hardhearted like the judge, so he will defend us to the end. (2) God is just, not corrupt like the judge. (3) God regards us as his chosen ones, not as bothersome, poor widows who can't pay bribes. (4) God doesn't have to be begged. (5) God knows the right timing for us. (6) God is sovereign. In summary, be constantly open to learn more about God through Bible study and fellowship with other believers.

Question 10.

The Pharisee	The Tax Collector
Confident of his own righteousness	Comes to God with nothing
Looks down on others	Doesn't compare himself with others but with God
Lists his religious accomplishments	Has no religious accomplishments to impress God with
Really has "I" trouble	Is aware only of his need for God's mercy

Study 20. Luke 18:15—19:10. The Nobodies God Wants in His Kingdom.
Purpose: To see and accept socially insignificant people as Jesus did—infinitely valuable to God.

General note. Studies twenty through twenty-two could be grouped under the heading "The King Clashes with the Establishment."

Question 1. Don't stay too long on this question. Children were considered unimportant in those days, loved but socially insignificant. So Jesus' words in 18:17 take on a startling meaning: as sinners wanting to enter God's kingdom,

we must see ourselves as children. Children know they are completely depen-
dent on adults. They gladly accept that "lower" status. They have to be trusting and obedient to survive. They have a sense of awe and wonder.

Question 2. The popular question the man asked (v. 18) is expressed by
Jesus and others in different ways (vv. 17, 24-26; compare also study sixteen).
Jesus' answer does not imply that the ticket to eternal life is selling all one's
possessions and giving to the poor, for he goes on to conclude, "Come, follow
me." This was a test of commitment for this particular man, and he failed. He
was still committed to his riches as his god. Whatever is first in our life is our
god (for example, social importance, professional position, gourmet food,
pleasure, sexual satisfaction, being fashionable, spiritual superiority).

Question 3. The Lord must be absolutely first in a disciple's life. The natural,
good things in life like loyalties to spouse and other relatives, or the security
of a home, are secondary. When they are second to Jesus, he rewards us with
multiplying these very "sacrifices" and assuring us of eternal life (vv. 29-30).

Question 4. Confusion about riches and their own politically messianic
agenda set the disciples up for selective hearing.

Question 5. He is one of only two people who ever call Jesus "Son of David."
(The Canaanite woman in Matthew 15:22 is the other.) Every good Jew knew
that Son of David was a messianic title, but not even his closest disciples used
it of Jesus. This filthy beggar keeps shouting it despite the crowd's rebuke.
(Mark 10:46 records his nickname of Bartimaeus, meaning "son of filth.")
Jesus is impressed with the beggar's unique messianic insight and his insistent
shouting above the crowd. And before this rejecting crowd Jesus commends
him for genuine faith.

Question 6. Jesus, of course, knows what the man wants (v. 38). But typically, he wants the man to articulate his faith (compare 5:12; 7:40-50; 8:30,
45-48; 9:12-20; 38-41). That makes for a personal relationship, not just a
magic act.

Question 7. Tax collectors had to be shrewd characters, operating between
their own Jewish people who hated them and their Roman employers who
despised them. They would have to be very clever and strong-willed to col-
lect/extort the maximum from people and hand over only the minimum to
Caesar. A chief tax collector in an affluent town like Jericho would top the
rest of his colleagues in corruption and hardness of character. Rich tax collectors still suffered social and religious ostracism. Their only friends were people like themselves and other moral outcasts.

Question 8. (1) Such a mentally active person would also think hard about
life. (2) He evidently had achieved materially what he wanted in life and was
still deeply dissatisfied. (3) His undignified way of seeing Jesus (note Luke's
humorous description) indicates he was highly motivated to see Jesus—at
least curious and apparently hopeful that life could be different. (4) His expe-

rience in quickly assessing people's characters informed him that Jesus was authentic. (5) After hearing Jesus, his decisive character led him to right practical decisions.

Question 9. (1) Jesus takes the initiative in going to the sinner. (2) He establishes a personal relationship with the sinner. (3) They quite evidently (between verses 7 and 8) had a long discussion by which Zacchaeus could understand what Jesus' good news meant and implied. (4) The sinner repents and vows to make restitution. (5) Jesus confirms his salvation publicly.

Study 21. Luke 19:11-48. Delusions About God's Kingdom.

Purpose: To rethink our expectations about God's kingdom and our place in it.

General note. Messianic phrases in verses 9-10 would have caught the people's ears—"today . . . salvation has come . . . son of Abraham . . . Son of Man . . . save." So Jesus quickly seeks to dispel false expectations of Israel's political independence right around the bend of that Jericho road. He reiterates that while the kingdom of God has indeed arrived, its consummation is in the future. Disciples must stop speculating and get on with their assigned work.

The audience would have initially recognized a parallel between the nobleman in Jesus' parable and Archelaus, the son of Herod the Great. He had gone to Rome to ask Caesar to appoint him king, not just tetrarch (a lesser ruler) over Judea. But he had been such a bad ruler that a Jewish delegation followed him to the capital and succeeded in persuading Caesar not to appoint him king. At this point in the parable, however, Jesus' listeners would have been shocked, for the nobleman in his parable returns as king!

Question 1. (1) Jesus is a nobleman with authority. (2) He is returning to his Father to receive his kingship. (3) He leaves each servant with something very valuable to be invested. (4) The leaders in Judea reject him as God's Son. (5) Jesus will publicly receive his kingship from God. (6) Upon his return King Jesus will call for an account of how each servant has put his money to work. (7) He will reward the wise investors fairly. (8) He will severely judge those who have failed to put his money to work. (9) The King will destroy his enemies.

Note that each servant is given one mina. Some Bible interpreters suggest that because it is the same amount this could mean the same gift of salvation given to every believer. In a similar parable (Mt 25:14-30) the servants are given various amounts, which some suggest could represent different abilities and spiritual gifts. In any case, both parables stress accountability.

Question 4. Don't interpret verse 26 quantitatively. Think of spiritual resources, like the fruit of the Spirit in Galatians 5:22-23. For example, the more you love, the easier it is to love. The more you exercise self-control, the more disciplined your life will be. The more you witness to Jesus and his salvation, the easier it becomes to help bring people into God's family. The opposite is also true: Don't love, and you will lose whatever love you did have. Don't exercise self-control, and you will lose whatever control you once had. God's gifts multiply in you when you invest them in wise choices and activities, or they disappear (atrophy) when not used at all. Use it or lose it!

Question 5. (1) A political kingdom of Israel is not right around the corner. (2) God's kingdom is far greater and more glorious than an earthly kingdom. (3) Jesus, whom they are rejecting, will return as King, universally acclaimed. (4) They will be destroyed. This harsh picture of the nobleman in verse 27 (and also vv. 22-24) does not mean God is cruel, but that his justice is supreme.

Question 6. Some possible answers include deeply pained, compassionate (vv. 41-44); angry, firm, courageous, purposeful (vv. 45-46); determined to keep teaching, popular with the people, unafraid of the officials (vv. 47-48).

Questions 7-8. It is good periodically to ask these kinds of questions, especially when there are some who, not familiar with the Bible, have genuine questions. The group climate should always be comfortable for any to share doubts.

Study 22. Luke 20:1—21:4. Rejection of God's Kingdom.

Purpose: To learn from Jesus to deal with opposition to our faith and witness.

Question 1. The issue of Jesus' authority was not new (see Lk 4:32, 36; 5:24; 9:1; 10:19). After all, he had no official rabbinic training, and he came from inferior Galilee. But these opponents were dishonest. They had ignored his miraculous works as a divine sign of authority. They had rejected his clear, well-reasoned, scripturally based teachings. They had demonstrated provincial prejudices (Jn 7:52), disregarding Isaiah 9:1. Now for political reasons they were refusing to answer Jesus' straightforward and relevant question. They show themselves intellectually dishonest.

Question 3. Twenty or so years before there had been a disastrous tax revolt. Jesus' opponents were trying to force him into either calling for another tax rebellion (which would be treason) or appearing to be pro-Roman (which would cause the masses to reject him). He corrects their wrong assumptions. First, he was not anti-Rome like his nationalistic disciples and the crowd that followed him. Second, he says citizens should support the government that protects and benefits them. It is not an either-or choice. For an expansion of Jesus' answer see Romans 13:1-7 and 1 Peter 2:13-17.

Questions 4-5. The pro-Roman Sadducees were a small but powerful aristocratic group. (They controlled the commerce at the temple [19:45-46].) As descendants of Aaron, the first high priest, they qualified as candidates to be high priests. Former high priests or male members of their families were called chief priests. They rejected any belief in angels, spirits or life after death (Acts 23:6-8). This explains why the teachers of the law (who evidently were Pharisees) liked Jesus' answer to the Sadducees.

Their error was to assume that the afterlife, which Jesus and the Pharisees believed in, would be the same as life on earth, where marriage and procreation are essential. As with angels, procreation won't be necessary in heaven. Marriage relationships will not be the same. (Like all other relationships, they will be transformed into something different and better in heaven.) Jesus shows from a book the Sadducees profess to accept (Ex 3:6) that their revered leader Moses believed in immortality (20:37-38)!

Question 7. The Jews believed that the Messiah would be King David's human descendant. So Jesus uses a familiar messianic text—Psalm 110:1—to argue also for the Messiah's deity. Again, they do not or will not answer his logical question (v. 44).

The second question should help people identify with Jesus. He did not go through life's crises mechanically like a battery-charged robot: "He has been tempted in every way just as we are. . . . Although he was a son, he learned obedience from what he suffered and, once made perfect [mature], he became the source of eternal salvation for all who obey him" (Hebrews 4:15; 5:8-9).

Question 8. If status quo in their privileged, powerful positions is most important, leaders will fight for that survival. It takes courage to make major changes. It's easier to go along with the majority; Satan uses them.

Question 10. Jesus values simple, quiet, not showy, focused, straight-from-the-heart faith that loves God and is convinced of his purposes in the world.

Study 23. Luke 21:5-38. Jesus' Predictions of the Last Days.

Purpose: To be better-prepared disciples as we face the increasing troubles in the world.

General note. Equally earnest Christians differ in their interpretations of these passages. Be firm where Jesus is firm, and be open-ended where the meaning is not clear to you. For instance, certain activities have always existed, and Jesus says that these are not signs of the end (vv. 8-9). Throughout this discourse, what is clear is Jesus' emphasis on moral preparation rather than calendar preoccupation Compare Matthew 24:36, 42 and 2 Peter 3:1-18.

Studies twenty-three through twenty-six could be grouped under the heading "God Has the Last Word."

Question 1. It is important to see the whole chapter in one reading. Divide it into paragraph readings by different individuals. The aim is to get the group warmed up to the text. But keep in mind people's impressions that you can refer to as you go along. The disciples' admiration for that particular temple was ironic, because it was built by King Herod whom the Jews hated. He built it with Jewish slave labor over a period of sixty years.

Question 2. The question is personal in application, and it might be hard to make the connection with Jesus' prophecy. Like the disciples, most people focus on the present earthly existence with little regard for the future realities that Jesus predicts here. The disciples were expecting Jesus to establish a political state freed from Rome. This explains the ongoing arguments among themselves about the highest cabinet positions in Jesus' new government. We also can be like them in having wrong ideas about the kingdom of God and therefore wrong expectations about our part in it.

Question 3. Some of the troubles that Jesus describes have characterized all of history (vv. 8-11). Acts records the disciples' powerful witness and persecutions just as he predicted (vv. 12-17). But Christians in the last two thousand years have also experienced such witness and persecutions.

Talk about signs and wonders can lead to exaggerated curiosity or sensationalism. Some people like speculation more than the hard, steady work of obeying God in practical matters that Jesus stresses here and in his conclusion. But this is not to discourage studies about God's signs; that's what this chapter is about.

Question 4. Here Jesus' main concern is that his disciples have the right mindset in these sufferings.

Question 6. (Use discretion with this more technical information, but it can be helpful for more advanced groups.) We say Jesus *seems* to be pointing to these as final signs just before he returns—more cosmic, more intense and catastrophic than previous ones. But the problem we face is that Jewish historians like Josephus, writing about the signs preceding the fall of Jerusalem in A.D. 70, uses cataclysmic language almost identical to Jesus' words about his return. So is Jesus describing similar signs for both events, one that is past for us (Jerusalem's fall) and the other still future (his return)? Possibly. In any case, he makes it clear that the signs game is not to be our preoccupation. Carrying on his ministries in the light of his personal return in glory should be our highest priority.

Question 7. Compared to other trees in Israel, a fig tree has the fewest leaves in the winter. So when its leaves do appear, it is obvious that the season is changing. Jesus is saying the signs of his near return are also that obvious if only people opened their eyes (compare 12:40-59). How near is near (see 2 Pet 3:3-9)?

Question 10. See the note for question 7 in study nineteen.

Study 24. Luke 22:1-46. Jesus, Our Passover Lamb.
Purpose: To appreciate more than ever that Jesus is "the Lamb of God who takes away the sin of the world," and to be able to participate in the new Passover more meaningfully.

Question 1. Observe how Luke describes them: "looking for some way to get rid of him . . . afraid of the people . . . delighted (with Judas's offer)." They're cowardly political animals, afraid to do the right thing and sneaky about the whole thing.

Question 2. Luke has more to say about Judas's betrayal than the other writers, as though he could not get over its horror. (1) Judas had more opportunity than most people to know God intimately and to be an important part of his kingdom. (2) Jesus had been good to him, even though he knew at least by the third year which of the Twelve would betray him. He still called him friend at the point of betrayal. (3) His betrayal is in stark contrast to Jesus' holy determination. (4) This was the very Son of God that he was betraying.

Judas is a clear example of how Satan works in people. He cannot work in a person's life without that person's permission. Judas's betrayal was the result of progressive deliberations (Jn 12:5-6). Peter's denial was due to weakness of character. Judas *regretted* his sin—and committed suicide. But Peter *repented* from his sin and was restored to fellowship and service with Jesus.

Question 4. This question should encourage probing of the study's stated purpose above. (For the origin of the Passover, see "Now or Later" at the end of this chapter.) (1) Jesus knew the prophecies about Messiah's mission, especially in Isaiah 52:13—53:12 and Jeremiah 31:31-33. John the Baptist had publicly proclaimed him as "the Lamb of God who takes way the sin of the world" (Jn 1:36). All this prepared him for his cosmic mission. It was not death that he wanted to avoid. It was the temporary separation from his Father when he would take into his body the sins of the world (Mt 27:45-46). (2) The Greek verb in verse 15 is intensive: "With desire have I desired to eat this Passover with you before I suffer." Can you feel his deep passion? But this was his reason for coming into the world: to establish the new covenant with humanity. And yet his closest friends did not understand what he said and what he was doing!

Question 5. These amazing verses are comparable to John 17:6-10 (Jesus' high priestly prayer in Gethsemane right after the meal). He has total confidence in them to be his leaders, carrying on the mission he has begun. Incredible! But after all, he did pray all night before he chose them (Lk 6:12). And he is confident that he has sufficiently taught and trained them, and that the Holy Spirit will be permanently within them (Jn 14:15-17, 25-26; 15:26; 16:5—all spoken that same night).

Question 6. Luke alone records this intimate dialogue with Simon Peter. There is no more touching scene with a failing disciple than this one. Don't rush through it. If people can identify with Simon here, they will better understand Jesus' heart for his bumbling disciple.

Question 9. (1) Have a customary place for praying (vv. 39-40). (2) Make it private with the Father (v. 41). (3) Open your heart to the Father (v. 42). (4) Be guided ultimately by a basic desire to do God's will, not your own (v.

42). (5) Let yourself be passionate as you focus in your praying (vv. 43-44). (6) There is a time to stop praying and move into action (vv. 45-46).

Study 25. Luke 22:47—23:56. God's Word from the Cross.
Purpose: To grasp the historical facts and implications of Jesus' death and to improve our communication of its meaning to others.
General note. Throughout the study anticipate the evangelistic possibilities of seekers responding more personally to the truth about Jesus. Close the group study in time and take the opportunity to speak personally with them. Be alert to the Spirit's gentle guidance.
Question 1. To Judas, Jesus is to the point but still friendly. To his followers he is firm in reprimand. To the high priest's servant Jesus is compassionate. To the arresting party Jesus is cool and calm.
Question 3. Possible reasons for Jesus' silence include: (1) Jesus knew they were not sincere in wanting to hear the truth. (2) Jesus refused to be simply an object of curiosity. (3) The Jewish leaders and Herod had heard enough truth from Jesus. (4) They would only twist his words as they had before. (5) Jesus knew their minds were already made up. (In V. Grieves, *The Trial of Jesus*, the British lawyer cites twelve flagrant illegalities in the arrest and trial of Jesus.)
Question 4. Pilate despised the Jews but had to play politics with them. Judea was the last assignment a Roman governor wanted, as it was known to be the most revolutionary prone in the empire. Had he freed Jesus, the frenzied crowd would have rioted.
Question 5. (1) The other Gospels say that both criminals began reviling him. One continued; the other one changed his attitude (see question 7). (2) The people in verse 35 seem neutral in Luke's picture, but the other Gospels include them in reviling Jesus. See verse 48 for a possible overlapping. (3) "The rulers even sneered at him." (4) The soldiers mock him. (5) The centurion gives evidence of faith in Jesus. (7) The crowd (v. 48), probably inhabitants of Jerusalem, is saddened. (They perhaps are not deeply interested in Jesus. Nevertheless, this prepares them for the apostles' evangelism fifty days later. See Acts 2—5.) "But all those who knew him, including the women who had followed him from Galilee, stood at a distance, watching these things" (v. 49).
Question 6. Luke has a keen appreciation for God's grace in salvation, and this is a dramatic example. To the very end Jesus is reaching out to hopeless people, especially those rejected by others. The man has been impressed with what he sees and hears from Jesus. He is a superb illustration of how far God's grace can reach—that there's no one so bad that God cannot save, and it's never too late when there is simple faith in him.
Question 7. Jesus' relationship with his Father remains consistent—totally trusting in God's sovereign purposes and care. His lifetime of trust in a loving sovereign Father stands fast in death.

Question 8. God's eternal plan to save his lost people was at last carried out in history. His death tore open the thick curtain between a holy God and a sinful people. There is no other way that we can come to God; only through Jesus dying as the sacrificial Lamb of God for us sinners.

Study 26. Luke 24. God's Word from the Empty Tomb.
Purpose: To let the clear historical facts of Jesus' resurrection strengthen our faith, and to move us out into the world in obedience to Jesus' resurrection commission.

Question 1. Luke's warm appreciation for the women in Jesus' ministry comes to focus in this last week. These are the ones "who had followed him from Galilee" and the "daughters of Jerusalem" (8:3; 23:27–28, 49). They remain a loyal group at the foot of the cross and watch his burial. After Jesus' ascension, we see them praying and also awaiting the Holy Spirit (Acts 1:14; 2:4).

Question 3. Some older translations and paintings have assumed that the two were men. For example, the RSV in verse 25 says, "O foolish men." The Greek, however, has no gender and is literally translated "O foolish ones." One is clearly a man, Cleopas (v. 18). The other could be Mrs. Mary Cleopas (see Jn 19:25; Clopas=Cleopas). In any case, they are typical of Jesus' followers at this point—deeply loyal, deeply caring and deeply disappointed.

Question 4. He's friendly. He's casually observant, noting them in serious, sad conversation. He certainly doesn't seem threatening, for the couple responds to him trustingly. He evidently has a sincere manner that encourages them to talk easily about what is heaviest on their heart.

Questions 5-9. These questions are intentionally personal and sometimes subjective. It is important that Jesus' resurrection does not remain only an interesting but irrelevant historic event. These questions aim at helping people to identify with people in the text and with Jesus himself. They give opportunity for people to express themselves candidly. (Imagine a seven-mile Bible study with Jesus!)

This prepares the group for the application questions. The aim is to provoke serious consideration about ongoing implications of Jesus' resurrection for the rest of our life. The resurrection and the commission of the Lord Jesus are inseparable!

Ada Lum teaches at the Bible Institute of Hawaii. She also visits various countries to do Bible study training for the International Fellowship of Evangelical Students. She is the author of Jesus the Disciplemaker *and* How to Begin an Evangelistic Bible Study.